FEELING BROKEN: SOLDIERS COME HOME

AN EXPLORATORY STUDY OF SOLDIERS WHO FEEL BROKEN POST COMBAT

BOBBIE DAVIS, PH.D., LCSW

authorHOUSE®

AuthorHouse™
1663 Liberty Drive
Bloomington, IN 47403
www.authorhouse.com
Phone: 1 (800) 839-8640

Melissa Dunn, MLIS Owner, Editor Writing Services

Published by AuthorHouse 12/20/2017

ISBN: 978-1-5462-1840-1 (sc)
ISBN: 978-1-5462-1838-8 (hc)
ISBN: 978-1-5462-1839-5 (e)

Library of Congress Control Number: 2017917860

Institute for Clinical Social Work

An Exploratory Study of Soldiers Who Feel Broken Post Combat

By

Bobbie M. Davis

A dissertation submitted to the faculty of

The Institute for Clinical Social Work

In partial fulfillment of the requirements for the degree of

Doctor of Philosophy

November 1, 2016

Abstract

This study explored former combat soldiers' self-descriptions of being "broken." All participants were solicited with a request to discuss their understanding, personal meanings, and events that led them to feeling broken. Participants were required to have deployed to either Iraq or Afghanistan and to have referred to themselves as being broken.

A grounded theory design was used to capture the complexities of the participants' combat and post combat experiences. Fifteen men volunteered to participate in up to four interviews.

Data analysis revealed six categories which were broken down into the five findings: Numbness results in withdrawal from relationships and social engagement; Experiencing death, witnessing death or injuries of people close to them, and realizing that they could get killed at any time; Idealization of command is promoted, but is invariably ruptured; Survival guilt is bad news; and Physically broken, mentally broken, and emotionally broken. Also addressed was the distinctive process that unfolded as the participants engaged the researcher around the exploration of being broken. Theoretical, research, and clinical implications are discussed.

For Jeremy, Dannie, and my mother and father

Acknowledgments

I have many people who have guided me on this journey. First, there was Dr. Dennis Shelby who met me while I was interviewing for the program and did not see a person with a disability. Dr. James Lampe gave me a lot of encouragement and believed in what I was doing in my therapy with the soldiers that we work with in a treatment case, as well as the challenges I faced as a therapist who is blind. Dr. Joan Servatius provided me with multiple skills as we worked through some very challenging cases in treatment consultation. She helped with insight into my own countertransferences, as well as how I worked through the treatment with the individuals in a case. Dr. Anita Bryce provided me with a knowledge base of skills that were able to be applied in treatment, as well as a caring approach to treatment. Col. Jeffery Yarvis joined my dissertation committee and was also my chief while I served as a civilian at Ft. Belvoir. The knowledge that he provided around deeper insight into the issues that solders face while deployed was beneficial and held dear to the approach I use when working with soldiers. For the soldier participants I appreciate the step they took to open up their experience in this research. This is a part of your life that has been shared for the better good of other soldiers. I can't thank you enough for the insight you have provided.

BMD

Contents

Chapter

Statement of Purpose
Significance of the Study for Clinical Social Work
Statement of the Problem to Be Studied and
Specific Objectives to Be Achieved
Trauma "Locations"
Posttraumatic Stress Disorder

Statement of Relevant Knowledge
Summary
Theoretical and Conceptual Framework
of the Proposed Study
Theoretical and Operational Definitions of Major Concepts
Statement of Assumptions

Study and Design
Scope of Study
Participants
Data Collection Methods and Instruments

Will Not Understand Things They Have Done
Better Off Being Alone
Push Away My Family
Life Here is Petty
Worry about Stupid Things When I Have Faced Death
Summary

Army and VA Therapists Are not Listening
Therapist Sticks to Structured Manual Therapy
Therapist and Family Can't Handle Real Trauma Stories
Only Understood by Other Military
Persons Who Have Been Deployed
Only Understood by People in the Same MOS
Summary

Brief Description of Findings
Theoretical Implications

Clinical Implications
Future Research

Appendices

List of Tables

List of Figures

INTRODUCTION

Statement of Purpose

The purpose of this research was to explore the intrapsychic and interpersonal experiences that contribute to the combat soldier's self-perception as "broken." This researcher first heard the term while working in an Adult Behavioral Health Clinic at Fort Campbell, Kentucky. Returning combat soldiers created and used the term "broken" to characterize their psychological condition as a result of combat experiences. It is necessary for clinicians to discover the vast psychological meanings within this term in order to appropriately serve this population.

Significance of the Study for Clinical Social Work

The researcher first heard the descriptor of being "broken" when it was used by a patient treated in her clinical practice. With this patient, therapeutic work focused on the meaning of feeling "broken" and was essential to understanding the constructs that comprised this term. The patient presented underlying thoughts of suicide, which led to the patient's hospitalization for approximately six weeks. As a result of this work, a class project was conducted to further investigate the therapeutic experience with soldiers who reported being "broken." The results of the class project, which consisted of interviewing three therapists working with soldiers who identified as "broken," indicated that the therapists were familiar with the term and proceeded to delineate a wide range of emotional phenomena as well as social, familial, and command interactions that were associated with the term. It is possible that the term "broken" has been in colloquial use in military circles for many years. Remarque (1928) used the term to describe the experience of soldiers in World War I: "We will be weary, broken, burned out, ruthless and without hope. We will not be able to find our way anymore…" (p. 254).

According to a Department of Defense (DOD) report from August 2012, there were 131 potential suicides of active duty soldiers. Eighty of these have been confirmed as suicides and 51 still remain under investigation (DOD, 2012). In 2011, the DOD also reported that 165 suicides had been confirmed, with none under investigation. Suicide has helped focus public concern for the mental health needs of returning soldiers. The researcher has observed a wide range of distress among this group. Some soldiers report feeling broken along with suicidal ideation while others do not; however, these individuals can be suffering from significant psychological symptoms.

A systematic study of the experiences of soldiers who report feeling broken provided an in-depth exploration of war-related distress and how it is experienced intrapsychically, interpersonally, and in the context of Army life. It also offered a phenomenological context for the relationship between suicidal ideation and war-related trauma or distress.

Statement of the Problem to Be Studied and Specific Objectives to Be Achieved

This researcher's interest in the topic centers around the population she worked with at the Army post on Fort Campbell, Kentucky. Many soldiers there have been through multiple deployments since joining the Army and since the war began in Afghanistan, moving into Iraq and continuing in Afghanistan. Some of them have deployed as many as eight times since the onset of the war. Many of these soldiers have endured injuries during these deployments, which present as physical, psychological, or coexisting in nature.

According to the RAND Study (Williamson & Mulhal, 2009), 68% of 33,000 soldiers experienced blast-related injuries (p. 1). Fourteen percent of the soldiers return from combat with symptoms of Posttraumatic Stress Disorder (PTSD), Traumatic Brain Injury (TBI), or Major Depressive Disorder (p. 5). It was reported that 30% of soldiers that return screen positive for PTSD and TBI symptoms (p. 6). The report was broken down to define the ranges of the three most prevalent psychological conditions: 14% PTSD, 14% Depression, and 19% TBI of the 30% returning with mental health symptoms (p. 6). Since September 11, 2011, more than 638,000 soldiers have deployed more than once (p. 6). According to the Army Mental Health Advisory Team, soldiers that deploy longer than six months or more than once are more likely to be diagnosed with a psychological injury (p. 6). It was stated that multiple deployments increase combat stress by 30% or more (p. 7). Overall, 17.2% of 80,000 soldiers screened positive for mental health immediately after returning from combat (p. 9).

This researcher's experience indicates that soldiers returning with either a physical condition or mental health condition use the term "broken" to describe their presenting issues and psychological state in general. This term is one that the soldiers have created and is commonly used among the soldiers at Fort Campbell, Kentucky. Although this term is used frequently, there is no consistent understanding of what meanings lay beneath the term. This research is aimed at an in-depth understanding of the descriptor "broken" as a summary statement regarding a grossly altered sense of self.

Emotional consequences of combat and life in a time of war are well documented in the literature (Fairbairn, 1952; Freud, 1920; Kardiner, 1941; Ornstein, 1994; Stolorow, 2002, 2007; Wolf, 1995). Combat often includes losses of fellow soldiers and commanders. It is important to note that psychological distress is experienced in the context of the soldier's unit, command structure, and family relationships. In addition to individual distress, the responses of command, fellow soldiers, and often family members to perceived emotional difficulties are all potentially linked to feeling "broken" (Mezei, 2012).

The objectives of this research were as follows: (a) to explore in depth the complex intrapsychic and interpersonal experiences that contribute to feeling "broken," (b) to generate a substantive theory about combat-related stress and its relationship to feeling "broken," (c) to compare and contrast the findings of this research with the trauma theories of Wolfe (1995) and Ornstein (1994), and (d) to provide a framework for clinicians working with war-related stress in active duty or veterans mental health facilities.

Trauma "Locations"

If it is assumed that "feeling broken" is an existential or a phenomenological expression of combat-related PTSD, or war-related distress, we must also be free to question our assumption about where trauma "resides." Does trauma only exist in the mind of the sufferer, or can it be found elsewhere? Contemporary trauma theorists have emphasized the relational, contextual, and mutual nature of trauma (Stolorow, 2007; Ulman & Brothers 1987). It can be said that trauma resides as a classification system in the *Diagnostic and Statistical Manual of Mental Disorders* (4th ed., text rev.; *DSM-IV-TR;* American Psychiatric Association [APA], 2000), or in a different classification system found in the *Psychoanalytic Diagnostic Manual* (PDM). It can also be said that trauma resides in the host of technical approaches that have evolved in response to the wars, and that it can be found in the contributions by Freud (1920), Fairbairn (1952), Kardiner (1941), Ornstein (1994), Wolf (1995), and Stolorow (2002, 2007).

The contextual and perhaps social nature of war-related trauma was observed at a war trauma conference held in Chicago (*The Emotional Wounds of War*, 2012). Several presenters made it clear that playing an active role in the conference was somehow helping them with dimensions of their war trauma. After the conference, several audience members expressed that they had experienced an activation and a reworking of some of their war trauma.

Data from a class project exploring clinicians understanding of soldiers who report "feeling broken" indicated that soldiers experienced a profound feeling of change in the way their command, fellow soldiers, and family interacted with them. Is this just an expression of a radically altered sense of self, or do individuals in the relational environment experience something about the identified war trauma "victim" and deal with him or her differently than they did in the past? Real life experience does not confine distress to the pages of a diagnostic manual, theoretical paper, or one person's isolated mind.

There has been an increase in soldiers starting the process of a Medical Evaluation Board (MEB) to aid in a medical discharge from the Army. This benefit allows the soldier to receive financial compensation for a physical or mental health diagnosis, potentially for life. The financial incentives that come with a diagnosis increase this potential for soldiers to go through MEB. However, the evaluation itself can be traumatic. Some soldiers are unable to endure the process as it often entails a detailed recounting of events. In addition, the MEB takes approximately one year from start to finish. However, the stigma remains that some soldiers who go through the MEB are malingering, in order to receive an Honorable Discharge, and are not truly impacted by the war trauma.

Posttraumatic Stress Disorder

Posttraumatic Stress Disorder (PTSD) is defined in the *DSM-IV-TR* (APA, 2000) as follows:

> The development of characteristic symptoms following exposure to an extreme traumatic stressor involving direct personal experience of an event that involves actual or threatened death or serious injury, or other threat to one's physical integrity; or witnessing an event that involves death, injury, or a threat to the physical integrity of another person; or learning about unexpected or violent death, serious harm, or threat of death or injury experienced by a family member or other close associate (Criterion A1). The person's response to the event must involve intense fear, helplessness, or horror (or in children, the response must involve disorganized or agitated behavior; Criterion A2). The characteristic symptoms resulting from the exposure to the extreme trauma include persistent experiencing of the traumatic event (Criterion B), persistent avoidance of stimuli associated with

the trauma and numbing of general responsiveness (Criterion C), and persistent symptoms of increased arousal (Criterion D). The full symptom picture must be present for more than one month (Criterion E), and the disturbance must cause clinically significant distress or impairment in social, occupational, or other important areas of functioning (Criterion F). (APA, 2000)

The *DSM-IV-TR* (APA, 2000) approaches diagnosis from the vantage point that symptoms reside only in the soldier's mind. This implies that no other part of that soldier's life is impacting the response to the traumatic incident. This presumption, however, does not explain why some soldiers have PTSD and others do not, despite being exposed to the same traumatic incident. The diagnosis of PTSD in the minds of clinicians and fellow soldiers has created an amplified public awareness of the plight of returning soldiers. However, as Williamson and Mulhal (2009) pointed out, only a small percentage of returning soldiers meet the diagnostic criteria for PTSD; therefore, many soldiers with psychological distress may be misdiagnosed by clinicians or unfairly identified by their fellow soldiers. Each of these thought locations, in part, have a unique meaning and contribution to the formation of PTSD. A diagnosis of war-related PTSD cannot be isolated from responses in the family, military, social, and political environments.

The findings of a class project (Mezei, 2010) indicated that there are multiple ways of "feeling broken." There were also indications that there are several influences that contribute to being "broken." More specifically, soldiers reported feeling "brokenness" internally, secondary to the responses from their command, their fellow soldiers, and their spouses.

The stance of this research was that "broken" is more than a psychological problem with an array of observable symptoms. It is an interpersonal, social, and economic issue. Each of these locations indicates that the multiple areas in the individual soldier's life have been impacted by the experience of being "broken," which broadens the meaning of the phenomena.

Despite the potential diagnosis based on presenting symptoms, the complex experience that needs to be explored in depth with soldiers in distress is not limited to diagnostic criteria. Clinicians participating in the class project interviews (Mezei, 2010) indicated that they each had a unique conceptualization of war trauma which influenced their understanding of soldiers' symptoms and distress. In addition to the individual theoretical conceptualizations of clinicians, the literature on vicarious trauma indicates that some patients evoke the clinicians' preexisting trauma while other patients can create a new traumatic experience (Rasmussan, 2012, p. 223).

In the researchers' work with war veterans, when soldiers are afforded the opportunity to tell their story and how the story is impacting their lives, the following diagnostic questioning has been used:

- Did you lose a fellow soldier in combat or an operational accident?
- How are you coping with the loss of your fellow soldier?
- What has been your experience of your unit and command?
- How is your family interacting with you and you with them?

These are all questions that encourage responses based on different locations that potentially contribute to the reported "brokenness." Thus, the open-ended style allows the person to explore the different locations that are impacting the symptoms, which are in the soldier's mind about the trauma, rather than the therapist completing a symptom checklist which does not promote contextual understanding.

This research on the soldier's experience of being "broken" holds the potential to bring forth a deeper understanding of the experience of war-related trauma. The hope is that it can allow for the understanding of the elements that play into symptoms and how intrapsychic, interpersonal, social, and potentially political dynamics are aiding in perseveration of symptoms. Ultimately, the goal of this study was to produce an in-depth exploration of the soldiers' experience that will assist clinicians in their day-to-day work with soldiers experiencing war trauma.

Literature Review

Statement of Relevant Knowledge

Psychoanalysis has made major contributions to war trauma. Beginning with World War I, psychoanalytic understanding of war-related trauma has continued to evolve and expand. A historical review of psychoanalytic contributions will be presented. Many of the earliest ideas continue to inform contemporary trauma theory. Given the complexity of the theories, a general summary of central features will be provided.

Freud (1920) referred to traumatic neurosis and "war neuroses" as "significant ailments that interrupt one's ability to satisfy psychological needs" (p. 11). *Beyond the Pleasure Principle* (Freud, 1920) is considered the classic paper on war-related trauma. Freud focused on trauma, repetition, resistance to remembering, and the mastery of traumatic events. He identified characteristics of traumatic neurosis and distinguished them from hysteria by presenting more subjective ailments and mitigating general mental capacities. Freud stated that in order to generate a traumatic neurosis, one must experience surprise through fright. He refuted the possibility of neurosis forming through the experience of anxiety alone; instead, he stated that the neurosis must develop from not being prepared for danger, hence fright (p. 15). Freud also explained that if a wound or injury is inflicted simultaneously with surprise or fright, then it is unlikely to develop into a traumatic neurosis (p. 15).

Freud (1920) felt that a sudden unanticipated shock or fright could rupture the stimulus barrier and create the traumatic experience. He believed that a person could become fixated on the moment of the breach. This is evident through dream analysis, in which the individual repeatedly reexperiences the trauma and thus awakens in fright, only to associate power and strength to the experience and inevitably reinforce the trauma. Freud further explored the repetition compulsion, similar to the repetitive pattern of dreams, and discovered that in a soldier, the recurring trauma plays out in nightmares and in daily thoughts. He explained that the events of the trauma are going through the soldier's mind at all times, while there is also considerable effort during waking hours devoted to not remembering. Within this continuous internal struggle with the trauma, a fear builds around the possibility that the memory could provoke survivor guilt in the soldier. Therefore, this repetition through dreams and unconscious thought creates the reluctance to open up and address the traumatic memory, inevitability increasing anxiety. However, Freud stated that he had doubts that a person who experiences traumatic neurosis is burdened with the memories in conscious thought; rather, he suggested that it may be more of a concern that one commits great effort to not thinking about the traumatic memory, which indirectly reinforces the neurosis. Freud's theory suggests that repressed memories could actually exonerate the person from blame or fault (Freud, 1920).

Related to clinical work, Freud (1920) stated that a person would rather fight than remember (p. 25) and explained that the resistance to remember is acted out by fighting against the memory. He suggested that the soldier needs to turn the passive experience of repeated involuntary evocation of the event into an active process of mastery in order to alleviate symptoms.

Freud (1920) stated that repeating the unpleasant experience helps the person to master the powerful impressions by being active rather than passive, thereby allowing the displeasure to preoccupy the psyche. Each repetition potentially promotes mastery over the displeasure by allowing the individual to work through it. Freud stated that the instinct is to restore earlier states of the person's normal condition. It is understood that the instinct is historically determined and will ultimately return to an earlier state. Freud explained that the aim of all life is death and a central instinct in life is to bring death. His theory explains that the instinct of self-preservation and self-assertion on mastery diminishes as the person gets closer to death; consequently, on this path toward death, it is natural for people to want to die how they would wish. Freud explained that the death instinct never ceases, and therefore is not satisfied. This lack of satisfaction or displeasure plays out in repetition. As there is no process by which the success of the displeasure can be resolved, Freud explained that the person can develop neurotic phobias. The development of such phobias is an attempt to flight from satisfaction of the instinct, giving a model of perfection.

Fairbairn (1943) examined Freud's theory and questioned the "nature and the fate of impulse" (p. 78) in regard to one's actions. He looked at neuroses and explored the phenomenon through his developing object relations theory. Fairbairn emphasized the importance of object relations in early psychoanalytic thought, which directly contrasted Freud. Fairbairn felt psychopathology should focus on "the object towards which the impulse is directed" (p. 60), rather than on the impulse followed by the ego. Fairbairn stated that the nature of one's object relationships can contribute to the development of psychopathology; as a result, he used this object relations framework to look at war neurosis.

Fairbairn's (1943) central focus was the nature of the repressed material. He explained that traditionally, Freud believed that one role of the ego was to carry out repressions through the superego. According to Fairbairn, object relationships are essential to understanding that the ego must hold repression as a good object in order to satisfy the superego. Furthermore, the superego represents a deposit from the early objects that became internalized objects, through which a relationship is established. In addition, this identification of the ego with the superego is rarely complete, which brings forth questions regarding the relationship between the ego and superego.

The manifestation of repression as a good object brings to question the nature of bad objects. According to Klein (as cited in Fairbairn, 1943), bad objects are present and found in the psyche. This relationship brings to light the possibility that the act of repression is actually the function of the good object for the ego; yet, the nature of the repression is inherent to the bad object (Fairbairn, 1943). According to Fairbairn (1943), Freud stressed that repressed memories are intolerable and evoke unpleasantness that results in ego defense. He further stated that libidinal memories are painful as well as repressed memories that are ridden with guilt; thus, the superego turns to the ego for internal defenses against impulses. Fairbairn distinguished that repression is neither the intolerable guilt nor the impulse of the memory, but rather a relation with the bad internalized object. Therefore, memories are repressed as a result of identification with bad internalized objects. Consequently, if impulses are directed toward bad objects, they too become negative, resulting in internalization of the impulse.

Fairbairn (1943) further suggested that traumatic release of bad objects is common, a release which is evident during psychoses of war. The traumatic release is characterized through the bad object being released during dreams, in which the release is played out and anxiety increases from the dream situation. Fairbairn stated that the repetition compulsion occurs in order to release bad objects from unconsciousness and repression is a means to relieve the distress of traumatic wartime experiences. Wartime trauma is relived through common repetitive dreams, such as being attacked by enemies or being bombed by enemy planes. Freud clearly differentiated that dreams are either wish fulfillment or traumatic dreams. The wish fulfillment dream presents in a symbolic desire of the wish, while the traumatic dream repeats the situation (Freud, 1920).

Fairbairn (1943) explained that the psychosis of war is essentially the breakdown of a soldier and his or her dependence on objects. During war, the dependent individual cannot find a substitute for accustomed objects, which leads to an exploitation of "infinitival dependence" (p. 80), proceeded by separation anxiety. However, given the severity of such an environment, a new dependence on the soldier's regime is relevant to the success of new objects or experience of bad objects. For instance, Fairbairn differentiated the experience of separation anxiety between a solider under a totalitarian regime compared to a soldier of democracy. Under a totalitarian regime, a soldier forms a new good object of the nation and is dependent on the success of the nation as a whole. If the regime fails, separation anxiety ensues with the solider, who then views the object as bad and begins to experience social collapse due to the lack of a good object during war. Conversely, soldiers of democracy still hold familial objects, and through these good objects, are able to justify effort during war. Such a distinction is noteworthy as to how a soldier may experience war psychosis under differing regimes. Regardless, the notion is constant in regard to the object: If the object remains good, the experience is unlikely to lead to psychosis, but if the object is viewed negatively, separation anxiety may create an environment or experience that inevitability leads to war psychosis.

In general, the superego plays an essential role during wartime. It provides defense against bad objects and an overall maintenance of good objects. Consequently, if the object relation is compromised during war, then repression is valued as a way to maintain consistency with the object. The return of bad objects implies a failure of repression and of moral defense, which results in the collapse of the superego and the displacement of the regime or army as the good object (Fairbairn, 1943). As a result, separation anxiety is replaced by acute anxiety and the untimely release of bad objects. In summary, in sharp contrast to Freud, Fairbairn (1943) felt that war-related traumatic symptoms were a result of the massive failure of repression and the flooding of the psyche by the return of bad objects.

Kardiner (1941) also focused on the distinction and understanding of traumatic neuroses of war. His work represents the evolving tradition of Ego Psychology. It is notable for the early application of the concept of the adaptive functioning of the ego. He compared this form of neurosis to the similar symptomology of hysteria and compulsion neurosis. He explained that neurosis is essentially related to personality and common character traits, such as concerns of self, status, and relations with others. Kardiner stated that the traumatic neurosis presents symptoms that are found in all cases of war neurosis. More specifically, traumatic neurosis is a "fixation phenomenon, accompanied by a repetitive process, with a group of secondary defense mechanisms" (Kardiner, 1941, p. 69).

In general, war strips a person from the normal protections of the ego that are typical of peacetime. Essentially, a soldier experiences physiological factors of war through the terrible encounters with weaponry or combat. These reactions include fatigue, hygiene issues, or a lack of sexual outlets. Though all soldiers experience these factors, it is the fixation or reaction formation that develops the neurosis. Therefore, those with an unstable system inevitably react through psychological defenses in order to stabilize these encounters.

Like Fairbairn (1952), Kardiner (1941) stated that the soldier's identification with the cause of war is subject to variation, thus leading to a variety of responses to war. These responses are related to the military regime and its rewards and punishments, and essentially the control of the soldier's perception of the cause of war, although the interest in the war may depend on the personal or narcissistic objectives of the soldier. Kardiner explained that in war, the soldier's ego ideal has a forced replacement with the group in order to reduce conflict and generate ambivalence toward necessary wartime action. The soldier can identify with the cause and the leaders to create ties with the group and to regulate the violence and anxiety released by the war. Consequently, the violence of war consists of great conflict, urgency, and succession of rapid events, which negatively impact adaptations (Kardiner, 1941).

Kardiner (1941) further explained that the trauma is synonymous to injury and is linked to the external stimuli that alter previous adaptations. More specifically, the injury is to the ego and results in an adaptation, which may become disorganized. Therefore, a "traumatic neurosis is a "type of adaptation in which no complete restitution takes place but the individual continues with a reduction of resources or a contradiction of the ego" (Kardiner, 1941, p. 79). In order to master the stimulus, there has to be a relationship between the external stimulus and the resources that are available to the soldier. Kardiner explained that the organization effort of restitution occurs by continuing protective devices on the event. One such protective device is inhibition; here, the result is to cease functioning, which results in the remaining symptoms becoming adaptive.

According to Kardiner (1941), the features of traumatic neurosis are fixation on the event, atypical dream life, and constricted general functioning with increased irritability and explosive aggressive reaction. Kardiner stated that repetitive "traumatic" dreams indicate a fixation to the trauma. He explained that the dream is an indication of the direction of the recovery and what took place during the trauma. He further stated that aggression is also related to irritability. The aggression manifests in the soldier after the trauma and may be displayed by physical methods. This may trigger repression in order to offset the experience of aggression and irritability. Kardiner explained that aggression is also associated with inhibitions. In general, this type of aggression is disorganized and therefore does not have an aim. Consequently, through repression, disintegration takes place and conflict then becomes associated with the outer rather than the internal world. In summary, Kardiner identified that traumatic neurosis is plagued with fixation on the event, repetitive dreams, irritability, a tendency toward aggression and violence, and an inhibition to cope with adaptations (p. 159). The essential feature of Kardiner's theory is a massive decrease in ego functioning and a failure to adapt, which are brought about by the repeated injury to the ego secondary to repeated overwhelming stimuli.

Ornstein (1994) approached trauma from the perspective of self-psychology and lived experience. It is important to note that her views were not informed by war trauma per se, but by life in WWII concentration camps. She stated that traumatic memory can threaten the sense of psychic continuity. Ornstein referred to Kohut's theory that it is not plausible to understand a person's inner world without placing them in the culture in which they grew up, and that discontinuity can decrease the sense of sameness and connection to one's world in general and one's life in particular. Ornstein looked at the manner in which the memory is viewed and worked with in psychoanalysis. She stated that historically, the way in which memories are dealt with has changed, and that this change has evolved to a hermeneutic narrative approach. In this model, the remembered event is given a new meaning in a new context. Referring to Schafer (1983), Ornstein asserted that gaps in a memory can be filled in and the event can be completely altered, a process referred to as recontextualization. Ornstein stated that the new psychoanalytic version of understanding trauma in the person's life depends on the analyst's theoretical orientation and is dependent on individual psychic structure. Regardless, the narrative account given by the individual becomes an account of the self, and disconnectedness from the analyst results in a loss of identity. This loss of identity can transform the experience into a mere sequence of events (Polkinhorne, 1991 as cited in Ornstein, 1994), thereby resulting in an inability to heal any splits between affect and memory.

Ornstein (1994) explained that memory integrates the diverse experience of a lived experience. She stated that lived experience takes place in real time and does not have a completed structure until that experience is over. She explained that affect is a form of personal knowledge and is difficult to put into words.

Ornstein (1994) further stated that a traumatic memory is not an episodic memory (p. 132). Traumatic memory consists of the fragments of the memory and intrudes into the conscious. These intrusions occur in the form of flashbacks or nightmares. However, the integration of the memory fragments into the rest of the psyche is imperative. The integration does not indicate that the fragments of the trauma will disappear, but rather that they will cease to be experienced as part of the organization of self. Thus, there is an obstacle in integrating the fragments into the self. Essentially, a conflict is built into the fragments as well as a fear that they will bring back the traumatic experience. However, Ornstein established that there is a domain in which the memory is articulated to oneself and integrated into other memories. The integration depends on the resolution of the dialectic, depending on the empathic milieu that is available for the difficult psychological task (Ornstein, 1994, p. 146).

Ornstein (1994) explained that in the process of the patient recounting the events of the traumatic situation, disavowal mechanisms become a defense. The mechanism splits reality while allowing for the belief in another situation to exist. The healing of the split is what is represented in later life. It plays a role in the integration of traumatic memories, which results in greater psychic continuity (Ornstein, 1994, p. 149).

Ornstein (1994) further discussed the healing of the split as the integration of the split memories as they are remembered. The process is the function of the therapeutic dialog, where the articulation, images, and reconstruction are taken on gently by the patient and the therapist. Thus, that which is remembered is done so through mutual integration of the past with the present. Ornstein explained that the fragments may be articulated in visual, auditory, or olfactory form, and can be described with little affect. She expressed that the disavowal mechanism is used to protect against retraumatization. Ornstein also stated that there is a risk of retraumatization when an indifferent or unempathic reception is experienced during retelling. It is important to understand that what the therapist hears is not based on a common experience, and that the nature of the material can cause the therapist to struggle with comprehension. Ornstein stated that the healing of the split may never be complete, but may become free of nightmares or other symptoms, and that the memory may always be painful. Integration of the traumatic memory is in progress once the pain, anger, sorrow, and grief replace the numbness (p. 124).

Wolf (1995) adopted a view similar to that of Ornstein (1994) and explained concepts of the self in his work on psychic trauma, which essentially rests on Freud's (1920) view of trauma as a rupture in the stimulus barrier. He began to look at the concept of psychic trauma and the causes and effects within. He also sought to understand the process that leads from etiological events to psychological ones. Wolf stated that one must rely on theoretical assumptions of the dynamics of the psychological process in order to understand what occurs from the situational trauma to the psychosocial trauma. In normal psychoanalytic theory, the understanding of the symptoms would be grounded in the assumption of the normal limit to the excitability of the ego. To explain this, Wolf referred to Freud (1920):

> Any excitation from the outside which are powerful enough to break through the protective shield is being traumatic. Normally underneath the protective shield the ego is able to discharge excitement that has been aroused or to bind it by repression or other defenses to maintain equilibrium. (p. 97)

In other words, the normal defenses that people use to protect themselves from a perceived harm to the self are used to block the awareness that the harm is taking place. Wolf stated that excessive stimulus is characterized by the ego's inability to master the excitement. The loss is considered a traumatic state, and the ego will automatically block perceptions to protect itself from overstimulation. The blocking activity is called the stimulus barrier. Wolf indicated that the failure of the stimulus barrier results in a true emergency (the traumatic state). Factors that constitute the ego's ability to master excitability are based on age, constitution, general health, past exposures, and present condition. Freud (1920) stated that underneath the protective shell, the ego is able to either discharge excitement that has been aroused or bind it by repression or other defenses to maintain equilibrium. Wolf suggested that trauma occurs when stimulation has overwhelmed the ego's protective shield and capacity and leaves it in a traumatized state.

Wolf (1995) defined a psychic trauma as an emotional wound or shock that creates substantial and lasting damage to the psychological development of a person, often leading to neurosis. This is derived from physical injury where structural damage to the body and development is caused by the sudden intrusion of an object or substance. Wolf referred to Freud's (1920) postulation that psychic trauma occurs when an individual experiences an increase of stimulus in a short time which is too powerful to process in a normal way, resulting in permanent disturbances. Freud further stated that a punitive protective shield against excess stimulation, the stimulus barrier in the case of trauma, is penetrated and exposes the psyche to more than it can handle (Wolf, 1995). The defenses at this point manifest into symptoms. Freud claimed that the most important defense is repression, which causes the danger to be pushed out of the way, and in response creates the symptoms, which can then be triggered by later events (Wolf, 1995).

Wolf (1995) also addressed the issue of what occurs in chronic trauma, which is common to most soldiers that have deployed to Iraq and Afghanistan. As stated, most soldiers have been on multiple deployments. Wolf stated that one who suffers from chronic repeated psychic trauma originating from shortcomings in responsiveness of long-lasting relationships is different from one who suffers from adult onset trauma. However, some people experiencing a traumatic incident in adulthood may also be suffering from a chronically unresponsive selfobject milieu.

Stolorow and Attwood (2002) looked at the concept of absoluteness (p. 97). Trauma occurs when everyday assumptions of being are challenged, if not shattered, and when life as one knows it radically changes (Stolorow, 2007; Stolorow, Attwood, & Orange, 2002). Stolorow (2007) identified a distinction between emotional trauma in adulthood and traumatic experiences that interfere with development. He stated that adult onset emotional trauma can disrupt previously established regulation of emotions and that trauma is repeatedly relived in the present. Trauma is frozen in psychic time, and consequently, time collapses. Like Ornstein (1994), Stolorow emphasized the role of empathic attunement between patient and therapist. Clinical work involves the reorganization of memory into the larger psychic functioning. Stolorow made a crucial distinction in that the memory is split off, not repressed (p. 157). For Stolorow, trauma results in a radically altered different reality, and as a result, one does not recover from trauma, but instead adjusts to a radically altered sense of self.

There is some controversy over the applicability of psychoanalytic theory to war-related trauma. Boulanger (2007) stated:

> There is currently no way of locating adult onset trauma in psychoanalytic discourse except in the margins, no theoretical framework in which to fit Jonah's reactions without recourse to prior pathology There is no way of making sense of Remarque's weary, broken combat veterans without appealing to overwhelming aggression and the death instinct, to intrapsychic conflict, or to developmental arrests. (p. 42)

One could argue that a "tension" exists in psychoanalytic theory between war creating a new trauma, or war reactivating old trauma, or some relationship between the two.

Summary

An extensive body of theoretical literature has evolved since psychoanalysis began to address the unique qualities of war-related trauma in response to the suffering observed by military physicians and psychiatrists, both during and after World War I. The developments of war trauma theory parallel the development of psychoanalytic theory and subsequent extensive wars and conflicts. Theories have evolved from Freud's emphasis on unexpected shock that overwhelms the psychic apparatus, to Fairbairn's emphasis on objects and the return of repressed "bad objects," to Kardiner's analysis of disrupted adaptive capacities of the ego, to Wolf and Ornstein's focus on the self and finally, to the more existential focus of Stolorow. As Boulonger (2007) pointed out, aggression is a theme present in most theories. Sometimes the mental apparatus is so compromised that difficulties processing aggression emerge, or the experience of aggression coming at the individual releases bad objects or injures the ego, or disrupts previously established ways of being. Clearly, the aggression experienced intrapsychically or in combat is a distinctive feature of war-related trauma.

Theoretical and Conceptual Framework of the Proposed Study

The researcher assumed that elements of all the previously detailed theories would have some degree of relevance to this study. Theoretical concepts from the perspective of self-psychology, specifically those of Wolf (1995) and Ornstein (1994), were used to interpret, compare, and contrast the findings of the data analysis. The emphasis was on the sense of self, disruptions to the sense of self, and adaptive and potentially maladaptive efforts on the soldier's part to manage the disruption. As previously stated, the researcher views war-related trauma within a complex social, interpersonal, and military command structure. Hence, attention was paid to reportedly helpful and unhelpful responses to the soldiers' distress emanating from the social and psychosocial environment.

Wolf (1995) stated that "psychological trauma is an emotional wound or shock that creates substantial and lasting damage to the psychological development of a person often leading to neurosis" (p. 204). It is therefore important to better understand how a soldier who has been exposed to combat trauma develops the self-description of "broken" as a result of the emotional wound or shock. The soldiers with whom the researcher has worked have frequently reported that they joined the Army to "better their futures." However, in my work with soldiers, many of them appear to be psychologically hungry for mirroring and twinship, as well as selfobject experiences. Idealizing needs are often engaged with skilled instructors and superiors. They often bring deep needs for idealization that are activated by the more experienced instructors and leaders in the unit and broader command structure. However, it appears that when these relationships do not meet the expectations of the soldier, potentially traumatic disappointment and trauma stemming from violent combat experiences become intermingled. Wolf explained that maintaining a psychical wholeness of the self becomes a precondition for surviving the most extensive trauma and such psychic wholeness depends on past experiences. He further stated that an establishment of an efficient, emergent continuum from one pole of self-configuration to the other represents the healthy, cohesive self. The two poles represent the iterations in the environment, the selfobjects, past and present. These selfobjects, past and present, subsequently become an aspect of the self, which is constantly being reconstructed out of iterations of the past with the present selfobjects (Wolf, 1995, p. 78). Wolf stated that trauma in development must be defined as the interaction that interfered with the establishment of the bipolar continuum. However, he acknowledged that adult onset trauma impacts self-structures that have already developed. His description is closely related to the researcher's own conceptions of what is occurring when soldiers use the term "broken."

Ornstein (1994) explained that the lived experience of the traumatic memory threatens psychic continuity, proposing that traumatic experience can create gaps in memory. Observations from the researcher's work with soldiers indicate that gaps in memories of events were often filled in with constructions that pointed to their sense of guilt or blame for the loss or injury of fellow combatants. Further observations suggest that many soldiers may suffer from symptoms of war-related trauma during deployment, but often wait until they have returned home to attempt to deal directly with their distress. It appears that the process of adding often erroneous information to memory gaps continues throughout the deployment and until they are engaged with a skilled and empathic clinician. In looking at the effects associated with trauma, Ornstein explained that the effects can be the personal knowledge that the sufferer cannot put into words. In addition, she asserted that conflicts can prevent the integration of memory fragments. Identifying areas of conflict can ultimately help the clinician guide the patient to identify and elucidate previously unintegrated experiences. Her approach to understanding and treating trauma ultimately rests on facilitating the mind's striving for coherence.

1. The major concepts that guided the interpretation of the final data analysis were drawn from the above authors and also included Wolf's (1995) concept of trauma as a psychic wound, preexisting self-structure, and ongoing need for idealizing, mirroring and twinship, and selfobject experiences. Ornstein's (1994) concepts include the following: (a) trauma as interfering with psychic continuity—the sense of self and sameness over time
2. Efforts to fill in gaps of memory with often extraneous data,
3. Decreasing symptomatology as gaps are filled in,

4. Retraumatization secondary to unempathic responses,
5. Treatment as promoting the mind's striving towards coherence, and
6. The tendency of soldiers to wait to approach traumatic events until the environment feels predictable and psychologically safe.

These specific concepts are imbedded within the theoretical framework of self-psychology. Kohut is considered the primary theorist for the psychology of the self. The self is a structure built within objects in the environment (i.e., parents or others around the child; Kohut, 1971; Siegel, 1996, p. 71). He claimed that selfobjects are objects the child experiences as part of the self, with a sense of the self that can be controlled (Kohut, 1971; Siegel, 1996). Kohut defined the self as the personal center of initiative. His initial conceptions were of a bipolar configuration, the Grandiose Self and the Idealized Parental Imago. The self develops cohesiveness within selfobject milieu, which Tolpin (2002) defined as a "psychological surround" (p. 202). Kohut and Wolf (1978) explained that pathology pertinent to the topic of this research occurs when the individual disavows overwhelming experiences, creating a unique self-disorder characterized by a vertical split. Empathic failures during childhood can result in a fragmented or disorganized self characterized by omnipotence or faulty ideals. Central to the idea of the self is that it exists in a state of self-cohesion or disorganization. The self can respond to overwhelming situations by temporarily or permanently becoming disorganized or fragmented. Empathic responses from trusted individuals can result in the disorganization being of a short duration (Shelby, 1992, p. 68).

Kohut (1971) delineated three discreet selfobject functions or needs. Idealizing needs relate to the child's need to be near a source of omnipotent strength. The child feels reassured by his or her psychological merger with a source of strength and calm. The developmental outcome of the internalization of idealizing functions is ideals that guide the self. Idealized transference occurs when the child sees the idealized other as perfect. The child will take goals upon him- or herself to idealize the parent. The child will then begin to merge and start to feel a part of the idealized parent. This merger between child and parent assists the child in his or her development (Kohut, 1971; Siegel, 1996). The idealizing self splits the narcissistic self into two poles, the Ideal Pole and the Narcissistic Self Pole.

The Ideal Pole holds the perfection in the parent. The Narcissistic Self Pole holds onto the belief that the self is perfect. The idealizing transference relates to the Ideal Self Pole due to the child maintaining the perfect parent to encourage self-growth and understanding that the self will make mistakes, but inevitably will be fine. Kohut explained that disappointment in the idealized selfobject, faulty ability of the parent to be idealized, or loss of the idealized parent results in difficulty forming needed idealizing relationships throughout development, difficulty in self-regulation, and in the case of death, depression (Kohut, 1971; Siegel, 1996).

Mirroring transference occurs when the object, command, or fellow soldier is experienced as a separate person. The individual begins to identify that the object is in fact separate and is not used as a part of him or her (Kohut, 1971). Frustrations can be felt in this process in response to the individual seeking approval from the command or fellow soldier in order to fulfill his or her exhibitionistic needs.

Kohut (1971) and Siegel (1996) described twinship needs as a fundamental sense of belonging to the human race. The need and ability to feel part of a group and a sense of likeness with other people are also considered central narcissistic needs. Military training emphasizes unit cohesion, the ability to work as a team, and reliance on other unit members. The researcher's clinical experience indicates that the deep bonds that form among unit members are highly valued. Feeling isolated from fellow soldiers uncomfortable with possible symptoms of PTSD is reported as highly distressing.

Transmuting internalization is the process of taking in selfobjects and their transformation into self-structures (Kohut, 1971; Siegel 1996). It is assumed that soldiers enter the military with varying self-structures. It is also assumed that considerable development can occur during the process of training and performing military operations. The researcher's clinical experience indicates that an additional aspect of military-related trauma is a complication in the ability to use available selfobjects. At a time of great psychological need and self-disorganization, many soldiers are not able to engage in a manner which would forestall further disorganization. Central to male soldiers' experience of military life is the idealizing mirroring transference of the Oedipal phase. Ornstein (1994) defined this unique transference configuration as the intense need for mirroring from the idealized same-sex parent, which she felt to be crucial to forming a solid sense of gender identity. In a broader application, it is a crucial dimension of learning complex new skills and being able to perform independently.

Ornstein (1994) referred to the concept of empathy and the assertion that unempathic responses are retraumatizing. Kohut (1978) defined empathy as "vicarious introspection" and stressed the unavailability of empathic selfobjects in childhood as the paramount traumatizing condition (Kohut, 1984, pp. 82-83; Wold, 1995, p. 212). Kohut (1971) further defined empathy as the process of recognition of one's self in the other. In short, the ability to grasp what another person is feeling or needing psychologically at a given moment in time. The researcher's observation of military training is that it can be quite empathic during training but not during mission execution. Failure of an idealized commander to recognize and respond to psychological distress can have a retraumatizing effect on the soldier.

This basic elaboration of self-psychological trauma theory and related concepts will guide the discussion of the findings of the data analysis. If the findings indicate that further conceptual elaboration is needed, additional references will be integrated into the discussion of central findings. In addition the elaboration will include the interpretation of the experiences that relate to the soldiers' brokenness.

Theoretical and Operational Definitions of Major Concepts

The following are key concepts:
- Charge of quarters: The command structure after hours.
- Combat soldier: An infantry or aviation combat engineer that closes with an enemy combatant.
- Combat trauma: A trauma that occurs while in a combat setting.
- Deployment: When military personnel move from their home duty station to a distant location of combat or peace-keeping operations.
- Malingering: A soldier that feigns injury to get out of work duties.
- Medical Evaluation Board (MEB): A medical review board which determines a soldier's ability to stay physical or mentally fit to remain in the service.

- Military Occupation Specialty (MOS): A specialized occupation that defines the job, combat, combat service, and support.
- Post exchange: A mini mall or chain of small stores on a military installation.
- Reintegration: The process by which a solider is brought back from a combat setting or peace-keeping operation, consisting of a 90-day period of counseling and medical evaluations.
- Self: The psychological center of initiative (Kohut, 1971) which develops over time and can exist in various states of cohesion or fragmentation.
- Shoppette: A convenient store located on a military installation.

Statement of Assumptions

1. I am "broken" is a summary statement, self-reference, and colloquial term among soldiers referring to a grossly altered sense of self.
2. Combat or war trauma is a unique form of trauma with wide-ranging emotional consequences. The complexities of war trauma have been discussed within a wide range of psychoanalytic theories beginning with World War I.
3. The personal experience of "brokenness" may be related to the formal diagnostic category of PTSD, but does not necessarily indicate symptoms that would result in the diagnosis.
4. Combat trauma, war neurosis, and PTSD are not unitary phenomena in terms of personal, lived experience, but have some commonalities and variations.
5. While most war trauma and PTSD theories focus on extreme events and consequences, the loss of psychologically significant individuals may also be a central factor. Soldiers participating in the study will be able to articulate their experience of "being broken."
6. The methodology will allow the researcher to capture and analyze the experience in depth.

7. The researcher will be able to interpret central themes and findings that emerge from data analysis with a self-psychological framework.

8. The researcher will be able to construct a substantive theory about soldiers who report "feeling broken" that will encompass individual, interpersonal, relational, and broad social and specific military command meanings.

METHODOLOGY

Study and Design

The researcher used grounded theory, developed by Glasser and Straus (1967), Strauss and Corbin (1998), and Corbin and Strauss (2008), in order to better understand the meaning of the term "broken." These authors explained that grounded theory is "theory that is derived from data," which is then "systematically gathered and analyzed through the research process" (p. 12). As a result, the process of data collection, analysis, and theory are set in close proximity to each other (Strauss & Corbin, 1998). The authors also stated that research begins with an area of study and allows the theory to emerge from the data. Theory derived from data is more likely to resemble the "reality" than is theory derived by putting together a series of concepts based upon experience or solely through speculation (Strauss & Corbin, 1998, p. 12). Therefore, grounded theory was chosen to obtain a deeper understanding and to develop theory around the meaning of "broken" among United States military combat soldiers. As a result, the understanding and insight from this research regarding the term "broken" helped to elaborate common, individual meanings and experiences of these soldiers. It was hoped that through careful analysis based on in-depth interviews, this research would lead to a more consistent and thorough understanding for professionals working with combat soldiers.

Scope of Study

The research was conducted in the field on Fort Campbell Army Installation in Fort Campbell, Kentucky. The initial contact and interviewing of the subjects was conducted in an assigned office at the Department of Social Work at Fort Campbell, Kentucky (see Letter of Support, Appendix F). For soldiers that were discharged from the military, interviews were conducted over Skype. The researcher conducted face-to-face interviews to reduce risk of a psychological reaction that may not be observed during a phone interview.

Subjects were initially recruited through flyers and news advertisements (see Appendix G). The advertisements were placed in the following locations:

- Fort Campbell newspaper, *The Currier*
- The consolidated *Battalion Charge of Quarter (CQ)*
- *The Post Exchange*
- Shoppette newspaper stands
- The main lobbies of the Blanchfield Army Community Hospital
- ClarksvilleNow.com
- Facebook

These recruitment procedures were an open sampling method (Strauss & Corbin, 1998). Consequently, with this method there was potential that some subjects may not have presented with symptoms that were within the focus of the research. Despite these recruitment concerns, it is noted that obtaining subjects through open sampling is cohesive within a grounded theory methodology (Strauss & Corbin, 1998). According to Strauss and Corbin (2007), open sampling is a process of sampling that is "open to those persons, places, and situations that will provide greater opportunity for discovery" (p. 206). The authors stated that if sampling is too structured or calculated, one may inadvertently skew results and impact theoretical discovery. Therefore, open sampling relies on practical and convenient sampling.

In open sampling, snowball sampling is experienced as a secondary process to acquire new participants. Snowball sampling is a technique where the researcher obtains knowledge of potential participants from people who know people who meet research interests or who are possibly referred by another participant in the study (Corbin & Strauss, 1998). Open sampling methods were used in this research; more specifically, the word-of-mouth method was used to obtain subjects (Corbin & Strauss, 2008). This occurred between social workers and colleagues working at Fort Campbell Army Installation in Fort Campbell, Kentucky.

Participants were recruited until the point of saturation was met (Strauss & Corbin, 1998). The sample or category is saturated "when no new information seems to emerge during coding." Furthermore, saturation occurs "when no new properties, dimensions, conditions, actions/interactions, or consequences are seen in the data" (Strauss & Corbin, 1998, p. 136). As recommended by these authors, the researcher used an ongoing process of data analysis. The researcher was able to recognize saturation due to the analysis after interviewing each participant.

Participants

The population from which the sample drawn was either active duty or retired soldiers in the United States military who have deployed into a combat zone and have reported they are "broken." The sample consisted of 15 male participants between the ages of 27 and 56 ($M = 38.7$, $SD = 8.4$). At the time of the research, females were not permitted in a combat Military Occupational Specialty (MOS); thus, females were not included in the sample. The sample was predominately White ($n = 12$, % = 80) and married ($n = 8$, % = 53). Demographic information for the sample is presented in Table 1. Regarding military characteristics of the sample (see Table 2), a range of MOS and ranks were represented. Military status also differed among participants (see Figure 1). There were a total of 28 deployments reported and the mean number of deployments was 1.9 ($SD = .64$). The majority of deployments were to Iraq (see Figure 2).

Table 1

Demographic Characteristics of Participants *(N = 15)*

Characteristic	*n*	%
Race		
Black/African American	1	7
White	12	80
Hispanic/Latino	1	7
Other	1	7
Marital Status		
Married	8	53
Separated or Divorced	5	33
Never Married	2	13

Table 2

Military Characteristics of Participants *(N = 15)*

Characteristic	*n*	%
Military Occupational Specialty (MOS)		
00Z	1	7
11 B	4	27
13 B	1	7
13 F	1	7
15 A	1	7
19 D	1	7
25 U	1	7
63 W	1	7
88 N	1	7
91 B	1	7
94 F	1	7
0331	1	7

Rank

CPT-03 (Captain)	1	7
SFC-E7 (Sergeant First Class)	2	13
SGT-E5 (Sergeant)	7	47
SMG-E9 (Sergeant Major)	1	7
SPC-E4 (Specialist)	1	7
SSG-E6 (Staff Sergeant)	3	20

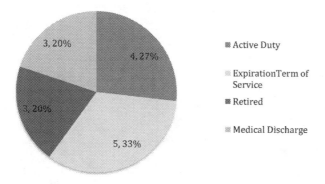

Figure 1. Number and percent of military status among participants (*N* = 28).

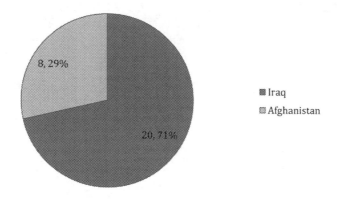

Figure 2. Number and percentage of deployments among participants (*N* = 28).

Data Collection Methods and Instruments

Study participants who responded to the recruitment flyer or who were referred were sent a copy of the IRB consent letter via email (see Appendix A). The letter fully described the study and listed the benefits and potential risks. Soldiers were asked to sign the consent form electronically once they decided to participate in the study. This was following their verbally having demonstrated an understanding of the research.

In the first interview, subjects were screened by phone to determine if they met the criteria (see Appendix B). Subjects were required to have had at least one deployment to Iraq or Afghanistan. The subjects also must have reported being "broken." Upon the screening the subject was also required to complete a brief demographic questionnaire (see Appendix C). This screening also included the scheduling for the second interview (see Appendix E), which was approximately 45 min in length. Subjects participated in a third interview approximately two to four weeks later. The researcher screened for severe symptomatology, acute suicidal ideation, depression, and social isolation that would indicate the participant being at a high risk for negative psychological reactions to the interview process (see Appendix D).

The researcher allowed for a fourth interview in which subjects could view the data collected and interpretations of the material, also known as "member checking" (Creswell, 2007). Essentially, member checking is a means to offer validation to the analysis of the findings, as well as gain additional data provided by the participants.

Data Analysis

Data were obtained and analyzed to arrive at the findings to operationalize and develop a substantive theory regarding the term "broken." As previously stated, each subject was screened for appropriateness. The researcher obtained consent to use a digital recorder to obtain the information reported by the soldiers during the interviews. The recording will be destroyed after the research is complete. Records were coded with a participant number.

To help protect anonymity, the names of the participants were stored separate from the data and kept locked in a file.

Data analysis occurred in several stages using a procedure previously developed by the researcher to accommodate the researcher's blindness. Each interview was transcribed from the audiotape to create a written transcription. The researcher reviewed each audio tape multiple times in order to listen for and identify themes as they emerged from the data. These themes were isolated from the transcripts and organized in an ongoing process of analysis which developed the themes into concepts.

Grounded theory emphasizes the "recursive nature of interviewing" (Glasser & Strauss, 1967, p. 74). Each interview leads to refined or further questions. It was assumed that additional questions would emerge over time. However, the following questions were asked of all participants:

1. Please tell me about your understanding of the term "broken?"
2. Have you heard other soldiers use the term?
3. Is it a term you apply to yourself?
4. How many times have you been deployed?
5. Was there a combat-related event that you felt changed by?
6. When did you start using the term "broken" to refer to yourself?
7. Were you ever disappointed in your command?
8. Did someone you were close to die in combat or an accident?
9. Please let me know if my questions have not addressed experiences that you feel are central to feeling "broken."

The process which accommodated the blindness of the researcher allowed the researcher to follow the steps of grounded theory analysis via listening, including open coding, which lead to axial coding, which resulted in selective coding. This process essentially refers to discerning themes which were then organized into categories, which were worked with until related categories emerged with a core category, with each category containing themes or properties that define it. Corbin and Strauss (1998) described this process as axial coding. Axial coding is the disaggregation of core themes during qualitative data analysis. Axial coding in grounded theory is the process of relating codes, categories, and concepts to each other, via a combination of inductive and deductive thinking.

The researcher used open-ended questions (see Appendix B). Open-ended questions and prompting questions are used to elicit more elaborate answers that will offer more content for data analysis. The developed questions allow for a fluid process during the interview, as further questions can be developed or removed to formulate or eliminate questions that are not pertinent (Strauss & Corbin, 1998).

Corbin and Strauss's method of constant comparison, the use of concepts and their development, theoretical sampling, and saturation were used in the research process to develop theory derived from the interview data. In addition, the researcher met regularly with her chair in a process Glasser and Strauss (1967) referred to as debriefing. This regular processing of interview data and the evolving substantive theory led to deeper data analysis and helped to insure rigor (Shelby, 2000; Shelby & Roldan, 2004).

The criteria that Corbin and Strauss (2008) identified were used in the evaluation process as follows: fit, applicability or usefulness of findings, concepts, contextualization of concepts, logic, depth, variation, creativity, variation, and evidence of memos. To judge the credibility of the study findings (Corbin & Strauss, 2008), the following questions were asked:

- Criterion 1: How was the original sample selected? How did later sampling occur?
- Criterion 2: What major categories emerged?
- Criterion 3: What were some of the events, incidents, and/or actions (indicators) that pointed to some of these major categories?
- Criterion 4: On the basis of what categories did theoretical sampling proceed?
- Criterion 5: What were some of the statements of relationships made during the analysis and on what grounds were they formulated and validated?
- Criterion 6: Were there instances when statements of relationships did not explain what was happening in the data (negative cases)?
- Criterion 7: How and why was the core category (if applicable) selected? On what grounds is the final analytic decisions made?
- Criterion 8: Are the concepts systematically related?
- Criterion 9: Is variation built into the theory?

- Criterion 10: Are the conditions and consequences built into the study and explained?
- Criterion 11: Has process been taken into account?
- Criterion 12: Do the theoretical findings seem significant, and to what extent is it entirely possible to complete a theory generating study?
- Criterion 13: Do the findings become part of the discussions and ideas exchanged among relevant social and professional groups?

The validity of the research is demonstrated through member checking. This process took place during the optional fourth interview with the research participants. According to Creswell (2007), member checking is the process by which the data, analysis, and interpretation of the research are brought to the research participants to judge the accuracy of the research data.

Limitations of the Research Plan

In general, measures of validity of a qualitative grounded theory study differ from those of quantitative research. As with true qualitative designs, the findings from this research are not generalizable to a larger sample. Despite this limitation, the study will provide deeper insight and understanding of the meaning of "broken" and the psychological implications for those reporting or using this term. Regardless of not generalizing the findings to a broader population, the benefits of this research are applicable to clinical work with soldiers.

As with any research, reliability is another essential factor to consider. In qualitative research, reliability refers to the stability of coding (Creswell, 2007). The researcher used a digital recorder to be consistent in gathering material from the participants. This ensured that statements during the interviews were not missed or overlooked. Codes were identified and used with each interview to ensure reliability of the data.

Protection of Human Subjects

Prior to advertising for subjects or conducting interviews, this study was approved by the Institutional Review Board of the Institute for Clinical Social Work and the United States Army. All participants received a written copy of the Informed Consent and were asked to convey their understanding of the content of the consent prior to participating in interviews. Participants were informed that they may stop the interview or their participation in the study at any time. Participants were monitored for signs of acute distress, suicidal tendencies, or acute mental illness. Participants reporting acute distress during an interview would have been escorted by the researcher to the Adult Behavioral Health Center, the Blanchfield Army Hospital Emergency Department, or the local Emergency Room, or the researcher would have contacted 911 for those participants who were interviewed over Skype. This research complied with the standards for human subject research established by the Institute for Clinical Social Work and the United States Army.

INTERVIEW PROCESS

The interviewer first contacted participants by phone in order to screen for their appropriateness for the study and to gather basic information. During the second interview, which was the first face-to-face interview, the participants were somewhat guarded. As the interviewer, I felt that the participants were assessing my ability to handle the information they would provide.

The participants were vague in the details they gave in the first interview. They limited the information they provided. One reason for this may be that during an initial meeting, whether for therapy or a research project, soldiers may limit the material to protect the listener from what they are going to tell them. Second, they may be protecting themselves from opening up too much and may be hesitant to be vulnerable with a new person. Third, they may not know how they themselves are going to react.

During the second interview, the participants seemed to rush in sharing their information and the time passed very quickly. The participants discussed facts and did not provide the emotional responses and details that they gave in the third interview.

By the time the participants reached the third interview, the experience changed. In the third interview, the participants opened up. Their emotional response was strong as they provided answers to the questions asked. They also reflected on the second interview and elaborated on the information they had provided.

The depth of the stories was profound in the third interview. The participants began to demonstrate an emotional response, giving thought to their reactions and telling multiple stories to describe their feelings.

In the third interview, the stories went beyond what the questions asked. This provided the depth needed for an analysis of data that was rich in nature and provided insight into the participants' experience of combat life, life after combat, and experience of being broken.

At this point in the interviews, participants were able to tell the story they wanted to tell, with no fear of judgment and no worry about their own reaction to the process. Working with soldiers in a therapeutic setting versus a research setting also appears to help them more fully open up when they are ready.

A form of disavowal was observed throughout the process. The participants often needed to split off their affect in order to answer the questions. At times, they would walk me through their experience and explain what led to the split in their affect. Other times, they would allow themselves to feel the emotions, and we would have to pause while they shed tears and expressed the anger that arose while sharing their story. This typically resulted in their sharing a different story or rationale as to why they were upset. They would then talk through the storm of emotions and distance themselves to ground their feelings.

A thorough analysis identified the categories which appeared throughout the interviews, as well as the properties contained within them. This process resulted in six categories.

The first category, The Event, contained the following properties: Which One Do I Talk About?, The Whole Thing Was Bad, and I'm a Killer. This category gave insight into the impact of deployment on participants and how deployment changed them internally.

The second category, Profoundly Changed, contained the following properties: Numb, Not Whole, Comparing Self-Ideals Pre and Post Combat, Others Don't See Me the Same, Afraid of Myself, and Not Feeling Normal. This category highlights the underlying self-ideals that occurred after feeling broken.

The third category, Survivor Guilt, was found throughout the interviews and encompassed the following properties: Holds Memories for Other Soldiers, The Story, It is My Fault, It Should Have Been Me, Keeps Building Up, and Handling Death. These properties were difficult for the soldiers to bring up and were not discussed until the third interview, once they felt comfortable expressing their raw emotions and vulnerability.

The fourth category, Command Support, revealed the following properties: Not Listening, Don't Understand, Being Let Down, Trusting with Safety, and Causing Loss. This category was replete with aggressive emotions, though participants stated that they were not broken by the command.

The fifth category, Relationship Distress, encompassed the following properties: Wife and Family Pose a Threat, Will Not Understand Things They Have Done, Better Off Being Alone, Push Away My Family, Life Here is Petty, and Worry About Stupid Things When I Have Faced Death. These properties arose throughout the interviews. The profound impact of the relationships was apparent and participants displayed significant discomfort while discussing these properties.

The sixth category was Not Heard. The properties identified were: Army and Veteran Association (VA) Therapists are not Listening, Therapist Sticks to Structured Manual Therapy, Therapist and Family Can't Handle It, Only Understood by Other Military People Who Have Deployed, and Only Understood by People in the Same MOS. This category related to participants' emotions about how they felt after returning from deployments and how their social environment impacted the way they felt about themselves.

The categories and properties will be discussed in depth in the next six chapters. Each category and property will be addressed and statements from the participants will be provided. These statements demonstrate the complex and raw emotions that participants felt and expressed during the interview process.

CATEGORY 1: THE EVENT

Participants had diverse responses to the category of The Event. They grouped their responses into different properties that described how they processed The Event that caused the feeling of being broken. The following properties were identified: Which One Do I Talk About?, The Whole Thing Was Bad, and I'm a Killer.

Which One Do I Talk About?

Regarding the property of Which One Do I Talk About?, one participant explained that there were multiple events which occurred that caused him to feel broken: "Multiple people died that I was close to, I don't want to pick just one." Another participant stated, "It was an accumulation of events from my first deployment."

Another participant discussed the first thing that happened and how this led into complicating other events in the deployments. He stated:

> Yeah. I'd have to say the thing that screwed me up was my friend getting killed. That and there was a lot of other stuff that continued on. There was [*sic*] a few people that I knew that was killed. Friends that were in the Army. It was kind of frustrating.

This participant went on to explain what happened after he was exposed to the deployments:

When it started to hit home it was like, yeah, we just got hit, some of the platoon got took by RPG, or got sniped, and you hit back. So the first tour was basically where I got my cherry busted. It was like, this shit is real, it's not like the movies or the video games, nothing like that. I would say I was naïve, but I knew what I was getting myself into, because I was over 30, 04-05, about 32. I say I didn't know, but I didn't know what war was, like actual war. First tour was an eye opener. It hit hard. It made me grow up faster. The word "broken" doesn't specifically mean PTSD, or oh God, I have seen some shit.

Another participant explained how the events pile on as the time spent in deployment increases, which does not leave time to process or work through the impact that the event had on the soldier:

There was a point when I was with the Iraqi army patrol and we hit an IED, the next day in a fire fight, my best friend got killed, the day after that I got blown up for the third time on that deployment. By a suicide bomber… A VBIED. It was a pretty bad couple of days.

This participant was unable to provide just one event, but explained how the experience started for him in his career as a soldier joining during war time:

I can't really give you just one. I was 18; I had no clue what I was doing. I knew what I signed up for; I did not have any illusions to that fact. I turned 19 when we invaded. Just this constant haze of stress even before we crossed the border because we were getting shot at by rockets from the other side.

He went on to discuss what happened as he faced the stressors of the events in the deployment:

I wasn't well versed in handling the stresses. I was a machine gunner at the time. I was on overwatch. I had a little bit of an episode; I snapped. I told them, "Fuck it, I don't care if they shoot me," [and] I told my SGT [Sergeant] to piss off. He walked up to me and clocked me across the jaw. Hardest I had ever been hit in my life. It was like something in me reset, clicked, "Okay, Roger, SGT [Sergeant]. I got right back to work.

One participant described how traumatic events impacted him in ways he believes will not change:

> I don't think it will ever go back. I guess because I have gone through such a tremendous amount of traumatic events that maybe the mind locks it away like it likes to do. The logical side takes steps, countermeasures, and it will help you survive. When the logic takes over, it is an easier existence when you think with emotion…starts clouding everything up, i.e., oh God, I can't do this, oh God, this is horrible, I can't think that way [*sic*].

Another participant who was injured during deployment described how the traumatic event changed his life in a way he did not anticipate:

> After almost dying, it caused me to take an outsider's looking assessment of myself, and after looking at what I was and who I was… I was almost like the stereotypical jock douche, an all-around cocky, arrogant, not approachable, very narcissistic, thought I was above everybody, and I was untouchable. I stepped on the IED and I didn't know what happened initially. I was on the ground; I didn't know I stepped on the bomb. I thought a mortar round landed behind me and tossed me. As soon as I looked down and saw that my leg was gone and how much blood was coming from me and able to identify it wasn't arteries [*sic*] blood that I was losing a mass amount of blood and that the likelihood of surviving with the sustained rate which I was losing blood…it was very obvious that the likelihood of surviving was slim to none. Even before the Med Evac [Medical Evacuation] got there…

This participant went on to describe his thought process during the incident which gives an insight into the shift in self-concept that took place after facing his possible death:

> My initial reaction to that was "Oh, fuck"; my secondary reaction was after the medic got to me, I looked at him and he was talking to me, I had him pull out a pen and paper and had him write my father's name and phone number so he could call my dad and explain to him what happened. So that my dad knew what happened and how I died. Rather than some BS letter from the Defense Department to inform my family that their son was killed after stepping on an IED. I wanted my dad to know all the details

so they could have a sense of closure. I was very certain I was going to die. The fact that I survived it made me change.

The Whole Thing Was Bad

In regard to the property of The Whole Thing Was Bad, the participants did not want to specify a part of the deployment that caused them to feel broken due to feeling like all aspects of the experience contributed to this feeling. One participant stated, "I did not think I would come back, so I didn't care," while another shared, "I only focused on my soldiers; my life didn't matter." One participant spoke about this feeling in depth:

> It would have to be where I got blown up playing yard darts. I didn't recognize it evidently, but anyone that was in my immediate circle noticed it within a month. That I was changing my personality, my demeanor, depression, only I wasn't depressed. I started taking on, I saw it as I was not going to die, and I was indestructible. I was the new super hero. So I started to volunteer for every outside the wire I could. Whether it was a diver, foot patrol, anything that put me out in harm's way. Because I thought I couldn't be hurt.

Participants also explained that the varying depths of the emotional experience of deployment relate to acceptance of their own death and the reality of others dying or of having to take another's life. One participant reported:

> It's kind of a desire to not be afraid to live. I've seen dead bodies and explosions, but I have never had to shoot anybody. I have had people in sights, and just waiting on the word, but that is just how it works.

Another participant spoke about the first time he was faced with combat and how the absolutism of the situation set in:

> The first time that we ever got fired on… We use to get rocketed all the time. There was an E-6 guy that was one of the Scouts, and we had been getting shot at. They had fired a whole bunch of rockets and they hit in front of the bunker… We [started] seeing smoke in the hole and a rocket came right over our head. And landed maybe 15 yards right in front of the TOC [Tactical Operations

Center]. We got pelted with rocks and smoke. At that point I felt like I was really, well, it really stuck with me. It was really when I saw it. That was the first moment that I felt I was in combat where it was like, wow. First I got the surreal feeling. You are in another country—you have never been anywhere like this before—and then it is just one of those things you're going to remember vividly for the rest of your life.

As participants began to talk about an event, they typically started to discuss other events which changed them as well. One participant shared:

It's kind of a desire to not be afraid to live. I've seen dead bodies and explosions, but I have never had to shoot anybody. I have had people in sights, and just waiting on the word, but that is just how it works.

This participant then described another event that changed him:

There were definitely some times where I let emotion get in the way of what was going on. I was the point man going through an in-tray way and I tripped and I actually landed on top of a guy with a knife, and after the room was cleared and I got up, I realized the knife was sticking in my body armor and I lost my mind. I went right after that guy. If it wasn't for my teammates, I would have killed that guy. [Faced with Own Death.] I would have beat him to death.

The participants explained that negative events that occurred during deployment could not be compared. One participant stated:

Each deployment was different. Anything that happened to you in combat is going to come back to you. I and a friend had to shoot this man down who was trying to get in the gate. We don't know why he was insistent in getting in the gate. We came to terms with it. Back then it was hard to come to terms with it, because we did not know if he was trying to get medical help for his family. I mean, what a man would do to try and help his family or to save a daughter or son. This man just went about it in the wrong way; we couldn't understand his language. Once he drew down on one of the grads with an automatic weapon, he had to be shot. That stuck with us for a long time. I was able to justify it because he went about it in the wrong way. It took me a couple of years; sometimes it is hard to justify things. Because you don't know why.

The participant then began to discuss another event that occurred:

> You can do things the right way or the wrong way. Every action has a consequence. That was the cleanup of Highway 8. There were a lot of cars just shot up by aircraft; we had to go in and clean it up. We had to get the bodies out, load them on large trucks, and stack bodies, stepping on dead bodies to stack more dead bodies, and then they would take them out to mass gravesites and bury them. It was a nasty, nasty job. The bodies had been in the heat for a long time and they would just pull apart. Sometimes you would grab an arm or leg and it would just come right off of it. That stuck with me in my dreams for a while, but I don't know how much it affected me.

Though this event was hard to process and difficult to put into perspective, the participant stated, "The thing that affected me the most was shooting that guy." This participant grappled with moral justification in the first event more so than in the second event. He was part of the cause of death in the first event, but not in the second event. Participants displayed a different response in regards to events in which they were faced with the choice and the rationale behind taking a life.

One participant then spoke about how the various aspects of his deployment impacted him differently. In addition, he discussed how these events triggered a heightened attention to safety and the realization that he is not invincible:

> The second deployment in Iraq, mission was field artillery; halfway through, mission changed and now we are security force. We are now doing infantry task. We had to go out in the town and do patrols, of a gas station. This caused the hyperalertness. While we were there, one of the soldiers gets shot in the back of the head. We never found the guy who did it. That affected me, because when I came back I have to know everyone who is coming around, what they were earn[ing], carrying... It took the death of the soldier to make us that hypervigilant in the deployment ad when we got back. We also had started highway patrols; this is what brought the alertness to the trashcans and potholes when I get home. There

was an overpass where we would take a break from patrol. The enemy had learned that this is where we hung out. They would wait for us to come and then they would throw grenades as they were driving over; they would wait until they had somebody down there to let them know we were all in there talking, then throw the grenade. It was a hope to get lucky. They injured two of the soldiers doing that, but they did not kill anyone. This was another thing I brought back, checking [the] overpass.

The participants shared how incidents are complicated in the aftermath of The Event and how this continues to impact them during and after deployments:

We did a lot of walking patrols. Now I am very careful about where I step. We had to watch for pressure plates; we lost a lot of soldiers to pressure plates. They usually lose one if not both legs. Everything they are carrying is a weapon or sensitive item. That goes up to a hundred miles away. Not only do you deal with your coworker or friend with two missing legs and gushing blood everywhere, you have to get him to have the golden hour to get ether terabits on him and back to get help of him being an amputee. Once the adrenaline from saving his life gets settled down, then you have to do police call and look for all the sensitive items. You can't leave anything behind. You have to get his limbs, his night vision; even if it is not considered sensitive, the Army does not let you leave it behind. You have to find his pictures from his wallet all that stuff… It is not so bad if you just think you're getting his things for his family, but you are thinking this IED just went off. There is a secondary or even a third line of IED that is trying to blow up first responders. So you're trying to find his personal effects in a mine field. This sends you into a greater effect of hypervigilance [and] then you bring this back here with you. I can tell you every gopher hole in my backyard because the gopher turned over some dirt; it stands out and I have them memorized. Sometimes it is hard to walk up on them, but I keep telling myself, it is a gopher hole.

An outlier in the research felt that he had greater self-insight, a stronger emotional connection to others, and was more willing to help others following his deployments, while most participants had shut themselves off, grown distanced from others, and become increasingly uncomfortable around people. This participant stated:

> I haven't had any combat experiences where I felt mentally or physically changed. I was who I am. As far as how I act. From the deployments, it has actually changed how I think about people. It has broadened how I feel about other people. And how I show emotions to friends and coworkers. Trying not to be distant from them or trying to be there for them as a support element and trying to understand what they have been through and listening more to them to help them if they are having issues.

However, the participant did discuss one change he went through in the very description he gave, which is that he became more aware of the impact that combat had on himself and his fellow soldiers.

I'm a Killer

The property of I'm a Killer was profound in the way the soldiers processed their self-concept after dealing with death in war. One participant spoke about how he processed the incident of killing a man while guarding the gate:

> I and a friend had to shoot this man down who was trying to get in the gate. We don't know why he was insistent in getting in the gate. We came to terms with it. Back then it was hard to come to terms with it, because we did not know if he was trying to get medical help for his family. I mean, what a man would do to try and help his family or to save a daughter or son.

This justification appears to be part of the process of understanding one's actions and trying to figure out if what one did was within the lines of protocol: "I was able to justify it because he went about it in the wrong way. It took me a couple of years sometimes it is hard to justify things. Because you don't know why."

Another participant discussed how he views killing others and explained that he does not feel any remorse after the act of killing in war:

> It didn't bother me. I shot a dude at point blank range. I don't

feel any remorse; I only can confirm one kill, and that's him. I've been a part of many kills, but I can't really say, "Yeah, I killed that dude." I shot in the area, you know, I was shooting mortars, you know, I was part of the contact. Except point [*sic*], he tried to grab my weapon, so I put two rounds in his chest.

Another participant spoke about how the shift from being "happy go lucky to a killer" occurred for him following his deployments:

They all impacted me. That is the whole point. It was okay with my people. Now that I am out, they jack with me. They don't understand. I'll hesitate quicker with a roach than a human. And just mutualize [*sic*] them. I don't mind killing a human because if they need to be killed, I will kill them. I don't have no compassion with them. I'm trying to get that feeling back, but before I was a soldier, I was a hunter. I was taught don't kill what you won't eat. I am beyond that now. I am a trained killer as artillery aircraft that is asked to come in and kill. It didn't matter when I did it then. I know what I am. I am such a happy-go-lucky person, so nobody knows. I am not understood and I know what I am. I am either good or bad. I am up on my game and a goofy old guy or I am scary evil. I don't want to be the scary evil, but you step into my world and be part of it, you're going to taste it.

Another participant described the first time he had to shoot and how this experience led to his comfort with shooting other individuals in war:

My first tour, or should I say the first time I got shot at, it scared the life out of me big time. We were all there; we learned what to do. And after the next time, the next time, and the next time it happened, it didn't scare me, it did not bother me, I didn't want to duck. It was carefree and I thought, "Let's do this," and I never thought I would be the reckless type in that way since.

He went on to explain his rationale for this change:

Part of it was the anger. I would say a lot of it. Somebody wanted to kill me because of what I was wearing. It didn't matter what religious belief was, or what I stand for, or the color of my skin. Simply for the fact that I had on that outfit and that flag on my shoulder somebody wanted me dead. I was enraged. So after I got past the initial shock of whizzing past my ear and this and that, and the other…the anger took over and it was just shoot. It became easier and easier, to the point when it just, not sounding weird, it doesn't bother me if somebody needs a killing, then fine. I believe in the difference between order and self-defense, but you know, if the situation dictates this guy is an aggressor and I am not going to run the other way, barricade myself, lock the door. You want to hurt me, I'm going to kill you. I'll put you down first, that is it. I didn't ever want to be that kind of person. I was reared in a very Christian home and values. I was not raised to be pushed around, but violence doesn't have to be the answer from my mom [sic]. Here I am, I don't want to talk you down, I want to hurt you first.

Summary

Discussing the events caused a flood of memories to occur. The participants rationalized the impact of each event in various ways in order to help them sort through the emotions and reactions that were expressed in this chapter. They relayed stories expressing internalization and self-blame, as well as justification and understanding, to the point of altering their self-concept in order to either hold on to the memories or to try and forget them.

CATEGORY 2: PROFOUNDLY CHANGED

The category of Profoundly Changed arose throughout the interviews. This category seemed to be the theme underlying the participants' experience of feeling broken. Profoundly Changed had the following properties: Numb, Not Whole, Comparing Self-Ideals with Pre and Post Combat, Others Don't See Me the Same, Afraid of Myself, and Not Feeling Normal.

Numb

Participants described this property in regard to an inability to feel their emotions or a fear of feeling their emotions. One participant shared, "You either get an explosion or instant shut down, and that's the acting out, the explosion." The participant explained that if he tries to feel the emotions, the emotions are not expressed in a way in which he is used to expressing them. The participant explained that when he allows himself to feel the emotions, he is flooded by them, which in turn causes him to be afraid of his feelings. Numbness keeps the soldiers from feeling the changes that have occurred or from remembering the things they have seen. One participant stated, "I could bottle it up as long as no one would ask me." This was further described as follows:

> Sometimes I don't feel anything. I don't feel like I feel anything. It's like it builds up and then all of a sudden, it just breaks. It

comes out and then I am back to that again. I think I make a breakthrough and then it all dams up again.

On the other hand, the participants tried to explain the reason why they numb themselves. One participant stated, "When I was drinking I wasn't able to control those feelings and it would end up with my crying and going off to be alone." This statement reflects the participant's response to people asking him about his deployments and how he was triggered due to not working through what he had seen and done while deployed.

One participant explained why maintaining a feeling of numbness is necessary while deployed:

Do what you have to do to live day to day and have all the emotions of being away from home. Because it's not where we want to be. It's not where I wanted to be. The only way for me to do the job I was doing was to tuck that away and not deal with it. The main concern was to get back home. I didn't feel like I could do that if I was distracted with my desire to be home. So I turned it off.

Compartmentalizing their experiences while they were deployed helped the participants continue the day-to-day exposure of the death of their fellow soldiers as well as the fear of their own death. One participant discussed when he remembered this change and how he reacted to the change.

It was funny to watch the transition because when we first get there, when a siren goes off everyone is like diving next to shit and running to bunkers. It was almost hilarious by the time we got to leave to watch the new units come in and deal with that kind of stuff while the rest of us were just walking around like everyday business. We didn't even bother to defend yourself [*sic*] at that point.

In an attempt to explain this action of maintaining a feeling of numbness, a participant answered the follow-up question regarding the nature of the fear of experiencing one's emotions: "The fear. The being put in a situation where my emotions take over and I am unable to react rationally. If that made sense."

Not Whole

Participants identified "Not Whole" as feeling like a part of who they used to be is missing. One participant reflected, "I do still consider myself broken or not whole; a piece of me is not there." Participants attempted to identify what caused a part of them to go missing, or expressed confusion about the reason why part of them is missing. One participant stated:

> You had a mission, you had a job, you a purpose, a direction and coming home something in that equation is missing. You separated from the service and you feel like there is huge piece that is not there anymore.

The participant explained how combat played a part in that which was missing. Other participants explained that they started to see this once they began to work after leaving the military. One participant explained, "As soon as I am not at work and not dealing with anything work related. I don't want to talk to anybody, I'm introverted, that was not a quality I possessed before." This was further described using a scenario wherein he recognized the part that was missing:

> One day I was sitting on my couch heavily medicated; I really couldn't move. I lost my job that day because I couldn't go to work. It wasn't that I couldn't, I literary did not care. I didn't care about consequences, I didn't care about going in there, I didn't care about letting anybody down, relieving my shift. My wife had come home and saw me in the same spot wearing the same thing, like I had not moved in 10 hours. That was when I kind of realized that I was broken I wasn't being the same and I needed to start getting help.

Participants spoke of trying to regain what they felt was missing. Some spoke of this as a tangible part of themselves they could get back; however, they attempted to fill this need outside of themselves. One participant stated, "I keep trying to help others to fill that gap within me."

Comparing Self-Ideals Pre and Post Combat

This property was found throughout the interviews. The participants compared self-ideals pre and post combat due to combat experiences. One participant stated:

> We were a part of something. There was always something bigger. Something that mattered, whether it wasn't politically right to the guy next to me, but you're constantly yearning to be part of something that isn't there anymore…brings a broken feeling.

This participant went on to explain the presence of feeling broken in his life:

> Broken in my world is that you can always be successful, but whatever damage has hurt you, you can never get over it. There is a sense of loss, failure, lack of accomplishment that you can never get over. Because of your choices in life, they put you into that particular place in which you feel broken. Unable to fulfill your dreams.

He also explained how he was a different person after the deployments: "It brings a very separated or detached feeling from who you think you are. Who you define yourself as for years."

Participants began to look at who they thought they were and how this viewpoint changed. One participant stated, "I used to be more optimistic and now I am more negative. I made great strides before my military career and since my military career. After my military career, I am never satisfied anymore." Another shared:

> I have always been the 100-plus PT guy. I have always been the top of the scale for fitness, my entire career, and then all of the sudden the rug was yanked out from under me. This was beneath me and my self-image. I wouldn't have quit, but I still push myself pretty hard.

Another participant stated that his definition of feeling broken could be explained by comparing his self-ideals:

> It is the inability of being who I use to be. You know, I shouldn't be or I should be like this. Before I was in the military, I used to laugh and joke and go out and do stuff. Now I just sit at home in my workshop.

Similar to this statement, another soldier shared how his personality had changed: "I wasn't like this. I wasn't afraid to go out in public. I wasn't afraid to do the things that I like to do." Another participant stated, "I use to laugh and joke, go out, have a good time with friends, now I have four people I talk to outside of my family. I just don't trust people." This reaction toward others is a response that was found throughout the interviews. The participants' sense of trust had shifted after they witnessed what human beings can do to one another in the act of combat. It appears that this shift generalized toward social systems and relationships once they returned to their normal environment. One participant stated, "I had trusted the people to do it right with me and they didn't. They were just being human. So I am broken; it hurts. Now I only see the trees, I don't see the forest." Another profound example of this shift was found in a participant's reaction to his children upon returning home:

> You know, so… It's just the changes that comes along with the experiences I have had. You know, the hard part for me is with my kids. I am still trying to feel the emotions. I love my kids, but when one of them tries to give me a hug, I just go, "Hey."

Another participant discussed his reaction after divorcing two wives: "Since my first deployment, I have been told I am difficult to live with, and I can see that." Another participant described soldiers that experience this change: "They have the Conan the Barbarian type mentality. When you can't perform at that level any longer, you lose that self-image, and so they refer to themselves as broken and say, 'I am broken.'" The confusion is compelling and difficult for the soldiers to sort through and understand. Another participant stated, "I got back from deployment. It was going smooth. Things were not the same. I don't know if I was angry or if I just became an a-hole." These soldiers experienced difficulty in feeling the same after being exposed to the intense emotions of loss, despair, and disappointment that they hold with them following deployment. One participant shared:

> I am broken because I can overcome stuff and come out on top of adversity, but do I feel like I have deteriorated from who I use to be—happy go lucky and nonchalant about stuff? I would say yeah, absolutely.

Others Don't See Me the Same

Participants described the property of Others Don't See Me the Same as the way in which they were treated differently than they were before the deployments. This was illustrated in one participant's statement: "You never want to be seen as weak. Broken usually becomes weak or incapable." This also contributes to the above property in that it touches on self-ideals; however, the perspective here is how other people will view them and the changes in how they feel about themselves. One participant shared, "We were literally asked one day by some of the faculty, 'How do you expect a bunch of broken individuals to graduate college?' Yet we were the guys that graduated with As and didn't drop out." Some of the participants would rationalize the reactions, as observed in the following statement: "It is interesting to feel like there is a conception out there that veterans are less than whole or broken." Others, however, described how it impacted them:

> I don't know what I should, how I should react or act with people. Lot of things people have as far as it being a big deal to them, I don't have or care about. I don't hold small talk conversations. Real world is not the same… I don't care.

These descriptions came up multiple times. Participants would explain how they had been exposed to more meaningful events, such as death, and that the people around them who are not military only want to talk about frivolous topics. In the words of one of the participants, "People want to tell me about new shoes coming out and I'm like, 'I don't care.'"

Participants also shared that their peers in the military viewed them as different as well. One participant explained that this reaction added to the feeling of being broken: "Once you are not able to do what the Army wants you to do, the coworkers are going to have to take up your slack. It is a resentment amongst your peers." This describes a perception that the soldier who feels broken is impacted by the way the command and his fellow soldiers perceive that brokenness. One of the participants who served in the higher ranks indicated that the perception of the soldiers whom he was leading also elevated his reaction to feeling broken, to the point that he would put himself at higher risk: "I got the chance to go out and lead soldiers. I violated my profile. So I could do this. I was never going to be able to do what I spent my entire adult life preparing to do." He further explained his reason for feeling this way: "Soldiers will not respect a senior leader who cannot lead. I was not allowed to go on runs with them."

Afraid of Myself

Participants expressed the property of "Afraid of Myself" as a fear of what they are capable of doing. One participant stated, "I'm a killer now and this won't change." Another participant explained how this feeling began in his training and ended up with him maintaining the feeling of being "evil." One participant explained:

> I'm trying to get that feeling back but before I was a soldier I was a hunter. I was taught don't kill what you won't eat. I am beyond that now. I am a trained killer as artillery aircraft that is asked to come in and kill. It didn't matter when I did it then. I know what I am. I am such a happy-go-lucky person, so nobody knows. I am not understood and I know what I am. I am either good or bad. I am up on my game and a goofy old guy or I am scary evil. I don't want to be the scary evil, but you step into my world and be part of it, you're going to taste it.

There is a component of this property that seems to make the participant feel safe by keeping people at a distance. This relates to the feeling of losing trust in the people in their lives as a result of witnessing what human beings are capable of doing to one another, as well as what they themselves have done in the line of duty. One participant stated, "If people knew what I think about them they wouldn't talk to me, they wouldn't mess with me. People have stolen from me and they have taken my dignity, my honor, and it was stolen." Participants also explained why the soldiers got to this point: "Some of the guys when you come to the part of the job that we do, kill...[they] are broken because your emotions do not come into play anymore." The participants conveyed this concept as a profound change that they do not fully grasp and, as such, they are unable to reintegrate back into their social norms. They feel changed by the act of killing in war and have become fearful of their ability to kill and how this taps into their aggression. One participant stated:

> You know, if the situation dictates this guy is an aggressor and I am not going to run the other way, barricade myself, lock the door. You want to hurt me; I'm going to kill you. I'll put you down first, that is it.

He went on to explain the process he goes through when questioning his actions:

> I didn't ever want to be that kind of person. I was reared in a very Christian home and values. I was not raised to be pushed around, but violence doesn't have to be the answer from my mom. Here I am, I don't want to talk you down, I want to hurt you first.

The participants' aggression was intense and they felt that it was justified. A participant explained his feeling after being injured in the combat zone.

> At first I was pretty blood thirsty. I wanted my prostatic device and get right back over there and lay them all to waste. I wanted retribution. It lasted about four months. The humbling was when I came to terms with I [*sic*] was not going to be able to jump right up put my device on, pull an M4, and go over and kill people.

He then described the shift that occurred: "When I realized my time in combat was done, I was in a new chapter of my life—a new experience and a new normal."

Not Feeling Normal

This property may blend into other properties above; however, it seems to be a specific property of Not Feeling Normal. One of the participants stated, "I can't find me anymore." Participants described the change in their feelings about who they are and how they react to life situations: "I have heard others say that they are cold or that they don't feel any more, and stuff in that line that terminology." One participant stated that he changed the way he processes day-to-day activities and no longer has an emotional response: "I only see things on the logical side. Right or wrong, it is how to handle the situation logically. I don't do anything emotionally, it is all calculated."

Soldiers who discussed the physical impact of combat and how they responded to the changes to their bodies after combat injuries offered a different perspective:

> I stepped on an IED and had my leg blown off. That would change a person pretty good. Physically that changed me, mentally that changed me. Let's not kid ourselves: Nobody goes through something like that without some level of change.

He shared the struggle of wearing a prostatic leg, but was more impacted by the loss of his ability to have children:

> I lost a lot of use in my left hand. I lost all hearing on the left side of my head. I lost, and this was the hard one for me, the ability to have children. That was the hard one. I can deal with not having a leg, but I wanted to be a father. That really hurt for me that I can't have kids.

These soldiers expressed the fact that the injuries they endured are not something they will simply "get over." These physical and mental injuries are interwoven into their very beings and inform the way in which they perceive themselves and the world in which they live.

Summary

Profoundly Changed was a compelling category that encompassed the following properties: Numb, Not Whole, Comparing Self-Ideals Pre and Post Combat, Others Don't See Me the Same, Afraid of Myself, and Not Feeling Normal. Each of these properties helped to define the participants' experiences of feeling broken. The descriptions throughout gave profound insight into the depth of their experiences and how these experiences have changed their perceptions of themselves and the world around them.

CATEGORY 3: SURVIVOR GUILT

The category of Survivor Guilt was present throughout the interviews. As the participants discussed different parts of the interview, the properties of Survivor Guilt arose. The following properties were identified in the interviews: Holds Memories for Other Soldiers, The Story, It is My Fault, It Should Have Been Me, Keeps Building Up, and Handling Death.

Holds Memories for Other Soldiers

The property of Holds Memories for Other Soldiers was a participant's response to honor the soldier, battle buddy, or friend who was lost. One participant stated, "I want to keep the good memories of the people I loved and live my life to the fullest." Another participant explained the way in which he and his friends honor a lost soldier:

> We all go out and celebrate the memory of my friend's life over his grave on his anniversary of his death, because he was such a great guy, so positive and full of energy that we never wanted to mourn him…so we celebrate and have a party on his grave.

Participants described several different types of ceremonials to honor the soldiers who were lost:

> His wish when he got back from deployment was to buy a Harley, so every time I start my Harley up, I look up to the sky and say,

"Let's go ride, buddy." There is that aspect that I don't forget him [*sic*]; every ride I tribute him that I do every day to him [*sic*]. Because he is not around.

The participant continued by stating:

I should live my life the way he would have wanted to live his. He is really good man. For me, I know he is looking down and I try to always make him proud. I loved him a lot.

Soldiers often indicated the nature of the psychological connection to the deceased soldier, which explains why they hold the memory.

The Stories

The property of The Stories was seen in the way participants would bring up the soldiers who they lost. One participant stated, "My best friend, he was the kind of guy that was hope for our future." The participants gave detailed backgrounds of the fallen soldiers and when they held those soldiers in such high respect. One participant shared, "He was the heart of the platoon. He was the guy in the platoon that would fight. He was liked by everybody, even the former squad, everybody liked him." Some participants also gave accounts of injuries these soldiers sustained:

One of our mechanics got hit with shrapnel, when we took mortars he got riddled with shrapnel. Me and BD had to carry him to the aids station while he was screaming for his mom. It is definitely an image I am stuck with. When I walked out of the medic tent, I realized I was covered in his blood. He was young; he was like 20-21. Married. That definitely changed my opinion on a lot of things.

Some of the participants distanced themselves by talking about how somebody else handled the loss:

I know one friend of mine. She was on a convoy and had a brand new soldier get killed. And she felt like if she could have done something different then he would be alive, which isn't true, But, that is where she is stuck and causing her problems all the time.

Participants not only described the details of the way the death occurred, but the psychological qualities of the person lost. One participant shared:

I have a friend that is both. He is physically and mentally broken. He lost his leg and other body parts and there is no bringing that back and he had to deal with that and will have to deal with that… he will never have the leg for the rest of his life. I was with him from the time they brought him in until they med evac [*sic*] him. I followed his process thorough his surgeries and even to today because he is not in the military. He does really good, but then he will have something happen in his life and he kind of goes into a low point. And then he reaches out to people he is close to and we all help him up in higher spirits.

The soldiers explained how they mirror their friends' personalities to hold on to the parts of those they admired. One participant shared:

My friends were who shaped who I am. The longer you are around them you start to take on their personalities. That is the kind of things [*sic*] that you keep with you. There is no reason that you should feel like you can't go on. Because Joe Bob died… He was a good dude and I am going to do things in his name.

Another soldier discussed how much of a sacrifice the soldier made as well as the qualities he carried from his father:

He was loved. Very loved. He was a good man. If you knew his story, you would be like, "Wow." His father was from Czechoslovakia, he literally jumped the frisking barbed wire fence, you know, during the Cold War. He literally escaped Czechoslovakia to get to America. He then volunteered for Vietnam. Because he thought he owed America, because he gained freedom. He then married a Czech in America. Joseph was his only son. His son wanted to be like his father since he joined, he wanted to serve his country. So his father sacrificed a lot for his country, giving his only son. His life.

It Is My Fault

The property of It Is My Fault was present throughout the interviews. Some of the soldiers were blunt in stating it was their fault, while others gave testament around the death of the individual. One participant stated, "I couldn't do anything about it. It impacted me tremendously; he was a good friend of mine." Offering an account of the information was important in order for participants to explain the basis for the feelings of guilt. Another participant explained, "We were clearing the building and he caught one in the shoulder and one in the head. I don't know what we didn't do right, you know, it just happened." Some of the participants stated it was their fault, but did not explain why. One participant was asked why he felt that his teammate's death was his fault, and his response was strategic: "I was in charge, I was the shot caller, I was the one directing traffic." This seemed to be a common way in which participants assumed responsibility for what happened. Another participant discussed his feeling responsible for the death of his friend while deployed: "He was in three or four years before I had got there, but we became friends very quickly. I always felt responsible because he wouldn't have gone if I wouldn't have agreed to go too. We talked each other into it." This participant further explained how the upper ranks felt responsible for the soldiers and how they felt when soldiers died in combat:

> I remember saying he is one of the best trained, and besides, he is with me, and telling this to their parents before we left. Promising that I would take care of them and then obviously they got killed. I did take those things to heart. Even though I was not with them, and there wasn't anything I could do. I still feel terrible. I still carry these with me.

One participant gave an account of a local walking up to the gate that he was guarding and trying to communicate that a child needed something. He then handed the child to the participant. He explained his reaction: "It really bothers me and it really messed with me because I didn't do CPR. I didn't try to revive the baby; I just gave it back to him. I didn't do anything with it; I just did that." The participant further explained how he holds himself responsible even though he knows he was following protocol.

In cases where participants did not assume responsibility for the death of a teammate, they instead tended to blame themselves for not emotionally engaging in the grieving process:

> I would feel bad for an instant, but then as the platoon SGT, I got too many things to do. So for me, I kept it off. Something was shocking, you want to show some emotions right then, and then

Bobbie Davis, Ph.D., LCSW

you remind yourself you have to keep everyone else safe, turn it off. So you turn it off and it runs the whole deployment. Then when you do open that box or bottle when you get back from deployment or that box opens while your drinking, it really sends you down a spiral. Then you go into the emotions of how could I have waited this long to grieve for this person, or feel bad they died... then think about their families and what an awful person I must be because I am not showing any emotions.

One participant explained why he reacted to death and injury in the same way: "I group the injured and the KIAs because it is the same. It takes you out of the fight. If somebody gets a serious wound, you med evac, you get them out as quickly as possible. You never see them again."

It Should Have Been Me

Throughout the interviews, the property of It Should Have Been Me consistently arose. The participants discussed the honor they held as well as the reasons why it should have been them. One participant shared:

Every day when I go to sleep, I think about what I did right and what I did wrong or what I should have done. And when I wake up it is the same thing. There are people in my life who are gone and should be alive. I shouldn't be here.

He further stated:

I feel like if I would have engaged enemies before maybe some people would still be alive. Maybe I shouldn't have called in the artillery to a particular location when I was angry, as opposed to when I was taking care of business.

The participants gave reasons why it should have been them. One participant stated:

The guys didn't deserve it. Part of me feels like it should have been me. One of the guys that got killed was in my truck...it would have been my truck; I was in the hospital...that was supposed to be my position. That was my spot, that was my truck, but I couldn't be there because I was in the hospital.

This participant explained how it was his fault that his guys were hit: "Somebody popped up in my line of fire and I wasn't looking. He shot a RPG at one of the vehicles." He later spoke of the impact of this incident and how the men treated him, adding to his own self-blame:

> Next several weeks, the guys in my platoon would not talk to me. I thought I was a dead man walking. I thought I would be hung out to dry or catch a bullet to the back because I had let them all down. They did not trust me.

A higher ranking participant talked about the responsibility he felt for the loss of soldiers who were killed by another soldier:

> I knew their name and their face, I knew if they were married, if they had kids; I mean, I knew them. They were a part of my team. Here is a guy that came into my family. I mean, these guys were a part of my family, like my second family. And [I] broke that trust and killed other soldiers. It changed me.

Keeps Building Up

The property Keeps Building Up was witnessed in participants' descriptions of how they honored the lost soldiers and retained feelings of guilt, adding to the feeling of being broken. One participant stated, "Absolutely this feeds into feeling broken; there is nothing else in the human race that makes me feel less human then not to being able to sympathize with someone in loss." Other participants shared how things changed for them. One participant stated, "I've either dealt out or dealt with more death than most people will see in their lifetime. After a while, you just get numb." Another participant shared, "Yeah, so there was [*sic*] a lot of things that change you. You become numb to life. You know, you refuse to accept happiness and certain things because you know something bad is going to happen."

Each of the participants described how the loss of a soldier or witnessing death played a part in their feeling broken. This participant explained how the process happened for him:

> Coming into work, driving down 124, you see a dead deer, you're like, "Oh, a dead deer," and you keep on driving. Imagine if it was

a dead body, would you stop, would you call the cops, you know what I mean?

He explained that the exposure of seeing death daily changed the way in which he processed death. The participant continued:

You see a lot of abnormal stuff so, you know, well in Iraq, I mean, it's an everyday occurrence. You see children walking by and there's a dead body, they are 5 to 6 years old, they are almost oblivious to it. They see it every day, so it's normal while walking to school. But for a 6- to 7-year-old American kid, that's a shock.

He then explained his reaction to death:

What do you want me to do, he's dead. You know, that's what I would say. That why somebody would say what is wrong with you, I would say, "I'm broken dude, what do you want me to do, somebody got killed, shit, what do you want me to do, cry?" It's not like a…you seen it so many times, it's nothing new, it's expected. If I see it now, it's like, tough shit. I'll get over it; you know, I'm not gonna freak out about it.

Although this participant described how he fragmented the way he processed death by shutting off his emotions, other participants proclaimed that they did not know how they were impacted by witnessing death. One participant stated:

We had to get the bodies out, load them on large trucks, and stack bodies, stepping on dead bodies to stack more dead bodies, and then they would take them out to mass gravesites and bury them. It was a nasty job. The bodies had been in the heat for a long time and they would just pull apart. Sometimes you would grab an arm or leg and it would just come right off of it. That stuck with me in my dreams for a while, but I don't know how much it affected me.

Another participant shared a similar anecdote regarding his response to a helicopter crash on a rooftop:

We carried him out and got him off the roof. He reached up to grab my buddy's hand because he was terrified, and when he reached back, all his skin stayed. They had to melt his wedding band off his hand. The heat of the flames melted it into his hand. You don't ever forget that. We had to start securing body parts and sensitive items. You never feel your humanity like you do when you're carrying somebody's arm and nothing else.

The imprint this places on the lives of the soldiers is profound and difficult to put into words, due to the depth of the emotions they expressed as they told their stories.

The loss of a fellow soldier is not easily resolved as the grieving process must take place much later than the loss itself. To put this into perspective, one participant gave an example of how a person might react to viewing death in a noncombat situation:

If you see a horrific wreck on the highway, you may stop, and if you see a dead body or limbs, you have time to sit there and go, "Oh my god, that is so bad." You have time to feel sorry for their family. You can start the grieving process right away.

Participants discussed the impact of having to wait to grieve. One participant stated:

Soldiers don't get that option at all. It's get back to work. Then, to compound it, that soldier's parts have to be picked up, his weapons have to be picked up, all the sensitive items, all his personal effects, and you have to detach yourself from it. That is the only way I can describe it.

Handling Death

Participants also commented on how they handled facing their own death or fear of their own death. This warranted a response similar to how they handled the loss of another individual. One participant stated:

You see your life flash before your eyes. It was kind of like the matrix. Everything is in slow motion, the wing grazed my leg and it hit the wall, and then we were in an hour-and-a-half three-sided ambush. It was traumatic, but...what was going through your mind...

Other participants spoke of the loss of the soldiers they fought with. One participant stated, "You got guys that you have trained with for over a year that you bled with and you wake up and they are gone." Another participant provided some rationale for his reactions:

They don't understand that when you live every day, and that siren goes off, and the mortar round or that damn rocket is coming in, you don't know if you're standing in that five meters. I would have rather went down and faced my enemy and had the opportunity to defend myself. Then to wonder every day for almost three years whether I was standing into that spot [*sic*].

Some participants also discussed an acceptance of fate and understanding of their own vulnerability. One participant stated:

I just got tired of running from it. If it was my time, it was my time, whether I got hit on the way to the bunker or the bunker got hit while I was in it, it didn't matter—I was still going to get hit, if it was my time.

One participant described his thought process: "It's not like a desire to die, it's kind of a desire to not be afraid to live," while another reflected on his own brush with death:

I was the point man going through an entrance way and I tripped and I actually landed on top of a guy with a knife, and after the room was cleared and I got up, I realized the knife was sticking in my body armor. And I lost my mind. I went right after that guy. If it wasn't for my teammates, I would have killed that guy. I would have beat him to death. And that's not [long pause], that is not rational.

Another participant felt that facing death was a humbling experience:

I learned an appreciation through my troubles and rehabilitation trying to get back up on two legs, having such a close call and almost dying. I just appreciate everything. It was an eye opening experience. As soon as the blast happened, it was an immediate realization that this shit is very real. I could still die very easily and everyone I love and who I am can cease to exist.

Participants illustrated the complexity of Survivor Guilt in that once a soldier takes his first life, it creates an emotional impasse inside that individual which allows him to continue taking the life of the enemy. One participant stated, "I've seen dead bodies and explosions, but I have never had to shoot anybody. I have had people in sights, and just waiting on the word, but that is just how it works." In this way, participants were able to disconnect from their emotions regarding what it felt like to have a person in their sights to kill. One participant described this process:

> The first time I got shot at, it scared the life out of me big time. We were all there; we learned what to do. And after the next time, the next time, and the next time it happened, it didn't scare me, it did not bother me, I didn't want to duck. It was carefree and I thought, "Let's do this," and I never thought I would be the reckless type since.

Another participant explained how this process happened for him:

> Part of it was the anger. I would say a lot of it. Somebody wanted to kill me because of what I was wearing. It did not matter what my religious belief was, or what I stand for, or the color of my skin. Simply for the fact that I had on that outfit and that flag on my shoulder, somebody wanted me dead. I was enraged. So after I got past the initial shock of whizzing past my ear and this, that, and the other, the anger took over and it was just shoot. It became easier and easier.

Summary

The participants processed Survivor Guilt in diverse ways. Their reactions and processes helped them to either understand it, block it out, distance themselves from it, or accept the death they witnessed or took part in. The properties of Holds Memories, The Story, It is My Fault, It Should Have Been Me, Keeps Building Up, and Handling Death provided insight into how Survivor Guilt complicates the feeling of being broken. The data provide insight into the potential complexity of Survivor Guilt. Soldiers are faced with not just one but multiple deaths.

Category 4: Command Support

The category of Command Support arose as participants discussed the incidents they were involved in while preparing for deployments, while in deployments, and after they had returned from deployments. The properties were stated as either adding to the feeling of broken or as being a part of the experience. The properties were as follows: Not Listening, Don't Understand, Being Let Down, Trusting with Safety, and Causing Loss.

Not Listening

The property of Not Listening arose as participants discussed the ideal properties that leadership should have. They gave multiple accounts of the command structure not listening to the lower ranking structure "on the ground." One participant shared:

> One of the reasons I almost died the first time was because my 1SG [First Sergeant] decided I was the 1SG's gunner. He decided to go, of course, on our planned route and we wound up hitting an IED. Obviously a bad decision, but you know, hindsight is always better.

Another participant described how the command failed to listen:

> When we got there we did not use the trucks, we used the MRAP [Mine Resistant Ambush Protected]. They were mine resistant. He preached no trucks. He never wanted the soldiers in trucks. He

wanted them out on foot going through these mine fields, because you never know when you're going to step on an IED. I would preach trucks. Let's at least take a truck. At least a truck in front and back if you want people walking, they can walk between the two trucks. We would have a way to evacuate, we got machine guns; there are so many advantages to the trucks. He didn't want them. I continued to use my trucks as much as I could. Matter of fact two of my trucks got blown up, and everybody walked away. Yeah the truck was destroyed, but the four people inside of it got out and walked away. Everything he did was for him.

Frustration regarding the command's decisions which lacked logic and had no tangible meaning to the soldiers was also evident. One participant stated:

Leadership needs to listen to the NCOs [Non Commissioned Officers] and they don't always do it. Officers at least don't always do it. In the military, we called it the dog and pony show. Everybody had to look pretty; everybody had to be dressed in the right dress. You know, we are invading a foreign country, why the hell do you care if I shave every day? As long as I don't grow a big scruffy beard, why do you care, to the point you make your SGT [Sergeant] watch me shave every day. It doesn't matter, nobody cares. Nobody except a couple of commanders and a couple of SMGs [Sergeant Major] that really want everybody to look pretty,... So, if everything is perfect, they get their next promotion or next reward.

This frustration was also described by one of the higher ranking participants:

My battalion had a secure of 1,000 sq. kilometers. It was a huge area, but mainly desert. It seemed like at least with my brigade commander had become [sic], you know when you would hear the weekly updates over the radio, it became a one up, i.e., my brigade sent this or my brigade's done that... It really doesn't, but it was like they were trying to one up their selves [sic] to general Petraeus. It seemed too petty. Why don't you just state what you did, and be judged by the merits of what you did? You don't have to expand it. That is one of the things I can't stand about people who are posers, as we call them. They rob the honor [of the] people.

Another participant stated the impact of the perception clearly: "You always have this image that your commander is, not a knight in shining armor, but there is a warrior or soldier code of honor, and you're not supposed to violate that." Another participant described an incident in which he felt the commander made a poor decision and pushed forward, resulting in his troop being injured:

> We did one where we went into a Taliban-controlled area. We would have had to have a brigade to get them out of there, but the commander wanted to go in and pull them back out. We start to go in and they get word. A guy says "Hey, you go around this corner, you're going to get ambushed." So the commander says, "Let's go." I said, "Sir, are you fucking serious? We are going to be ambushed any second. That is what we don't do." But, oh no. We are on a one-way street between a cliff and a wall. So we go over and as sure as the last truck turns, they hit us with armor piercing. Rounds. They started disabling vehicles and one guy gets shot. The commander is standing over them like a fucking nob.

Don't Understand

The property of Don't Understand was expressed throughout the interviews in regards to decisions made by the command. Participants shared their confusion as to why certain decisions were made and how they impacted morale. One participant stated:

> It got more strenuous and strict. Last tour, the SMG and Battalion Commander was just like… It was just too political correctness [*sic*], games, the way they ran it was just awful. It was frustrating, angry. We lost good men because of these strenuous rules.

Another participant talked about the reasons for war and how he believes that war is not treated like war due to the Rules of Engagement:

> There is no such thing as limits to war. It is either total war or no war. When you put these limitations, police actions, they are the most draining for personnel for morale. They are the worst. It just destroys morale. If you put a soldier and say fight to win, you win, regardless if you got one bullet or a sword.

Participants also spoke about how the command did not understand the impact their home life had on them while they were deployed:

> When I was in Afghanistan I had family issues crop up. And I thought the command was a little dispassionate or disconcerted, I guess. They just didn't, in my particular incident, they just weren't, I guess it was the aspect of, there wasn't any like communication of my command at any level to sit down with me and acknowledge, "Okay, we understand you are having these issues, and we are going to help you out as best we can." It was just kind of like they were ignoring, "Go back to work and do your thing."

Participants also expressed that the command lacked understanding and how this negatively affected the soldiers. One participant stated:

> It really had a negative impact because it was like, you know you're trying to give it your all, you're trying to keep it right there, but when it gets to a certain point… You need somebody to acknowledge that there is something other than being there in the zone, and that really never happened. Of course, when the issues really got blown up all out of proportion, then I felt like it was turned back against me. Like it was my fault, and it really hurt. I guess it helped that I came out from under that chain of command, after that event, because I didn't have no confidence whatsoever that they cared anything about the soldiers besides just what we were doing over there [*sic*].

The soldiers turned to their command for the emotional support they needed to get through the experiences of war and to process the loss of their home life they left behind. However, many participants commented that they did not receive this support and that it had a significant impact on their deployment experience. However, some participants also stated that the command was doing the best it could, given the situation at hand. One participant stated:

> The guys we lost, you always hold the command responsible, the shoulda, woulda, coulda, why didn't we do this, and it just takes time, and they were working with the info they had. During the line of duty, sometimes people die.

Participants also expressed their tendency to look back at the situations they endured in an attempt to process the aftermath. One participant reflected, "There is the second guessing of the command, then you get a leadership position, and the commander says 'I don't give a shit, this is what you're doing.'"

Some participants stated they were unsure whether their negative experiences with their command were central to feeling broken. One participant stated:

> I don't think it plays a whole lot into being broken. Maybe the feeling of loss of control. That is one of the biggest things I am still working on. Realizing and understanding that we don't all have the control. It is one of my biggest fights. Accepting that I don't have control on a lot of things and letting that make me emotional down range and while at home. The emotion is still overwhelming, it's still there.

Participants also reflected on their careers and the good they did, as well as the way in which their careers impacted their feeling broken due to the way they felt the command viewed their contributions to the deployments. One participant stated:

> I don't know if it is connecting to me feeling broken. There is a decided underwhelming feeling when I look at my personal packet and look at the stuff I earned and I think, man that is kind of pathetic. I only got the automatic awards. When there was a meeting, that was one of the questions that would come up; why is a LT [Lieutenant] that sits on a FOB [Forward Operating Base] getting a bronze star and the PV [Private] who goes and gets shot at several days a week given an ARCOM [Army Commendation Medal]? These feed into me feeling like I did not do much good, or that I did not do good enough to be recognized.

Being Let Down

The participants brought up the property Being Let Down during the course of many interviews. They discussed the disappointments and how they fed back into the lack of leadership in the command support. One participant stated: "My brokenness came from my unit. I felt let down."

Another participant explained his point of view about the Army and how the command changed this view through their leadership:

> What I liked about the army was, regardless of your upbringing, your morals, your philosophical views, political views, [or] religious views, you were one, you know. One Army, one platoon. And I kind of noticed it a lot and my chain of command was very political. If they didn't think you were going to be good for them, they didn't take care of you.

An example was given to understand the origin of this viewpoint:

> We had one SMG [Sergeant Major], he was ordering pizza... I was the COP [Combat Out Post] during that fire fight, I was in that particular fire fight. Any ways... We got hit, so forth, but uh... That particular time he was ordering food for himself and his entourage. They were eating Pizza Hut, Burger King, green beans, and all this shit, ordering from a PA Medic [Physician Assistant Medic] on a Black Hawk mind you. The rest of the battalion is eating MREs [Meals Ready to Eat] with the fucking rats in the dark. So it was very demoralizing.

Another soldier stated:

> You know, do your job, blah blah blah, but they were more concerned about getting the Internet, a gym, making the COP into a freaking FOB [Forward Operating Base], other than actually doing their mission. Trying to treat it like Garrison in a freaking combat zone. I don't know what they were thinking of, but anyway, it was very frustrating. It was the SMG [Sergeant Major] and above. It was very bad for leadership.

Another participant described the way in which the command criticized the soldiers' work while they were performing strenuous duties:

> My command had us working 12-hour days, standing in little metal boxes, looking out over the desert. They got as much sleep as they needed, they got to go to the chow hall, they got to work out as much as they wanted to, and then they would run around and yell at us for not having enough discipline, after standing in these hot metal boxes for 12 hours at a time. It was really discouraging. I'm out there in full combat gear in 110 degrees, and they are running up with just a helmet on, and yell [*sic*] that this place

needs to be cleaner and you need to stand up straighter. That was very hard for me to handle. I understand I was an E-3 and they were all much higher, but at the same time it is like, you could have taken over a shift here and there and given your guys a break.

One participant disliked the commander because of how he treated the people under him:

He would just cause a mess. The XO [Executive Officer] pretty much saved him his job. I loved everybody else; he was just one I didn't care for. He did not care for his soldiers. He didn't teach you to be better; he only cared for his OER [Officers Evaluations Report]. If I could avoid talking to that dude, I did my best to stay away from him.

Another participant discussed how the command treated the soldiers who were on the ground:

Our platoon was not allowed to go eat in the chow hall. Because we were always out on mission our uniforms were always dirty. Because we were dirty and we were forced to live in tents and not have buildings to live in, we lived in really rough conditions. So we were always filthy. They told us we were not allowed to eat into their chow hall. And usually they would, and I say usually because sometimes they forgot, they would bring us leftovers. That man was so obese it wasn't funny. That fat ass said we didn't need to eat in the chow hall because we stunk.

Participants described their leadership in one of two ways: Either their command inspired them to fight for each other or it caused them to feel defeated. One participant described the positive impact of the command: "ROE commanders, leadership plays a big role in morale, and basically how to win [*sic*]. You can be erupting or ill equipped, you know, low grade equipment, but if you have high morale you can win a war." Another participant addressed how the command was good for soldiers: "The lower level command was really good for structure for the younger leaders and the soldiers to see that the command actually cared about them. The people in charge actually cared about me." This description clarifies how leaders' compassion can encourage and strengthen the soldiers as well as motivate their efforts. "The 1SG [First Sergeant] really helped me out and I reflected on my time in the Army and my adult life and decided it was time to change my perspective. It was where I started to be more optimistic."

Trusting with Safety

Trusting with Safety is a property that highlights the physical and psychological feelings of safety. Participants discussed the faith they placed in their leadership and how this process led to either trusting their command structure or being frustrated with their command structure. One participant stated:

> It's very difficult, I mean you're in a very difficult position, especially in combat. You have to trust, regardless if you like each other or not, you have to trust the person whether he's above you or below you, as well as the guy next to you.

The participants explained why trust is important and how trust began the process of feeling either a positive or negative connection to the command and the unit. One participant shared, "Your chain of command got to take care of you [*sic*]. A soldier's going to do what you tell them to do. Your peer is going to watch the right flank while you watch the center, vice versa. It's a lot of trust you know." Another participant discussed his leaders' lack of training and its impact on his sense of safety:

> The one real major one was putting people in charge that had no experience in the field or in theater. Fresh off the plane and put them in charge of a QRF or patrol. You just don't do that. Either officer or enlisted. Whether you're noncommissioned or commissioned, if you have no experience, you're worse than PVT [Private] Stuffy. He's been there for a while; he has an upper hand. It is a big disappointment when they say you're going to do this. Well, teach them then.

Participants also discussed their confusion regarding some command decisions related to placing soldiers in harm's way. One participant stated:

> We as a battalion had lost 22, not to mention all the ones who got hurt. I personally experienced calling in for air support or tanks, and they would deny me and say there are too many civilians around, or no you're going to have to battle this one out or come

on back—there are too many people around there. I was really upset because I thought they were placing value on somebody's life over my soldiers. That was very disappointing for me. Putting my guys in more danger, where they could have pointed us in the right direction, but did not trust us enough to do that. They wanted to try and keep a good relationship with the locals or whatever. I don't know, I don't quite understand.

The soldiers in the study explained that their lack of trust in their command to keep them safe resulted in much confusion about why they were doing the missions and risking their own lives as well as their teammates' lives. One participant expressed the command "kicking him aside" to do another mission and described a feeling of "being lost":

They took a pair of us from the same area and kicked us aside to another group who was from Germany and attached us to them and left us and didn't check on us or anything like that. It was just our mission. We were assigned to them. The chain didn't really check up on us or have anything like that [*sic*]. He just threw us to the wind, for about five months. We were doing out own thing and were pretty much just left alone.

Another participant described how the command did not check up on them:

Our own COL and SMG not coming to see us for a whole year. We were on an outlying FOB [Forward Operation Base]. They would go here, go there, but never come down to see us to ensure we had mail or food. It got to the point [where] we had to trade cans of fuel to locals for a goat and humanitarian aids that we gave them so we could eat.

Participants also compared their command to that of other deployments:

Our commander was, there isn't a word to explain how just pathetic of a human being he is. Misuse of funds for his own personal comfort. You got 35 guys sleeping in a small room, sleeping on top of each other, but he had a building to himself. Just seeing him fail people over and over and it going beyond simple feelings. When [it] starts to affect health and morale and the ability to eat, that's very disappointing.

Causing Loss

The property of Causing Loss arose throughout the interviews. Participants provided reasons for the loss they felt as a result of the mission they were given. One participant stated:

> It got more strenuous and strict. Last tour the SMG [Sergeant Major] and Battalion Commander was just like…it was just too political correctness, games [*sic*]; the way they ran it was just awful. It was frustrating, angry. We lost good men because of these strenuous rules.

Participants directly blamed the command and then described the reason behind blaming them. One participant shared:

> He sacrificed his whole battalion to get these high ratings is the way I look at it. Not only that, he volunteered us for the deadliest area of operation that even the other infantry commanders would not take. We were stuck in the nastiest part of Afghanistan, within our own area of operation. Nobody had ever walked these lands before. We replaced a platoon at an outpost with a battery. He had volunteered us for all of that. I blame that commander for the deaths of those men. Because he would not listen. It was his way or no way.

Another participant provided an additional example to express his frustration with the command's attitudes and how these attitudes led to the death of the soldiers:

> All of his knowledge was about him being a great commander. About him going down in the record book for taking the most land, for being able to do this with an artillery battalion, and he did not care about soldiers. There might be some that were close to him, but for the mass majority, he ruined many officers' carriers. He ruined many NCOs' careers. He got a lot of people killed. If it would have been a different war at a different time, somebody would have fragged [killed] him.

One participant stated that he got into a fight with the LT: "Some hot shit LT straight out of school thought he knew better than I did and he got one of my guys shot over it." One high ranking participant discussed a time when he did not agree with the command's choice, and due to the command's choice, lives were lost:

> There was a big shooting incident down there. Our squadron commander got his PP hurt and called out. He said he wanted the regimental commander to make the decision. Our regimental commander was nowhere. So now our infantry guys were waiting for an hour, so they were tired of waiting and they wanted to go get their scout and pushed out. So everyone was engaged, but we were air support and we were not authorized to go. One of the guys heard on the radio that the troop commander got shot in the head; he was killed. Two other troopers got shot. There were seven or eight casualties.

Several participants stated that their command would take actions to win the glory, even if they put their soldiers at risk: One participant shared:

> We train for years and years to be tactical and [follow the] time-honored tradition as far as fighting in combat, but then you get there and these guys get their glory boy syndrome and they get guys killed. It is always command. The fact is, you sacrifice the blood of your men to get promoted.

Another participant stated:

> Then they had a bunch of guys killed in D Co. by a blue burka. She had a S-Vest [Suicide Vest] but they couldn't search her as a female. She walked up between them and detonated. She killed four and wounded one.

Participants also felt that their command was responsible for loss of life. One participant shared his view that the command failed to follow procedures that insured safety, resulting in loss of life:

> In the first two weeks, five guys [were] killed; one of them was the 1SG of the A Co. [Alpha Company]. He was killed because the Brigade commander put his truck first instead of the route clearance team, which would have saved his life inevitably because the route clearance team would have taken the blast which their vehicles are designed to do, and the Humvee is not. Everyone was turned to dust except the gunner. He died from the overpressure. Then they had us in the river for a week looking for one of the guys and we found [him] six inches below the neck.

Summary

In summary, participants viewed Command Support as either a needed source of assistance that provided them with the ability to manage their deployment experience, or as a component that caused significant disruption in their views of themselves as soldiers and their reasoning for being deployed. The experience of the Command Support provided or took away from the ideals of being a soldier and/or gave participants the needed structures to handle the multitude of tragedy experienced in war. The properties of Not Listening, Don't Understand, Being Let Down, Trusting with Safety, and Causing Loss provided insight into the complexity of soldiers' interactions with their command while in a state of war. Feelings of disappointment, betrayal, and willingness to sacrifice lives for personal glory were intense and at times bitter. The lines between technical leadership—the ability to direct a mission in an effective and "safe" manner—and being a target of idealization were often blurred. As the narratives indicate, it is sometimes difficult to sort out a leader's psychological experience and his or her technical capabilities. The data do indicate that a reasonable degree of idealization enhances the individual experience of psychological and physical safety.

CATEGORY 5: RELATIONSHIP DISTRESS

The category of Relationship Distress defined an aspect of the self-changes that the participants experienced as they deployed multiple times. This category highlights the impact of combat on soldiers' lives around family, relationship partners, children, battle buddies, and social functioning. The properties identified were Wife and Family Pose a Threat, Will Not Understand Things They Have Done, Better Off Being Alone, Push Away My Family, Life Here is Petty, and Worry About Stupid Things When I Have Faced Death. The participants reported that these properties related to their feeling of being broken. The properties were discussed with intense emotion, which set them apart from previous categories.

Wife and Family Pose a Threat

Participants described Wife and Family Pose a Threat as a reaction to how they felt while deployed and during reintegration. This property gave depth to the impact that family has on soldiers' decision making while in combat, either to protect themselves and return home or to put themselves in full combat and risk not coming home. One participant stated:

> So I didn't have to think about how much I missed my family, the wife, how scared I was [and] how I missed my kids my dogs. All those kind of things could not be a part of what I was doing.

Another participant explained how the stressors of his marital relationship began to add to the stressors of deployment:

> One little thing added in like me and the wife starting to fight, then I start seeing the symptoms showing up. Then more stresses are added, then another, and pretty soon I am not sleeping, I am just doing guard duty almost all night long. To get away from that stuff you start drinking. Just so you can get away from all that stuff.

Participants reported that the same conflict present in deployment was also present after they returned home.

Another participant explained the threat that family can present to soldiers while deployed:

> To a degree, you put the brick wall up 10 feet high and nobody can get to you. You cannot be over there worrying about [what] your son is doing and wonder what my wife is doing and if she is being faithful. You have to worry about what is in front of you right now. But when you get home, that spouse, they don't need the robot; they need whoever you were to them back then.

Will Not Understand Things They Have Done

Will Not Understand Things They Have Done is a property that overlaps with the category of Not Heard in Chapter 4. Participants discussed their feelings around not being understood by others who have not engaged in combat. One participant talked about how his wife and family did not understand his reaction to a family member getting hurt:

> My wife, family members, and so forth… You go back home and you find out your cousin had been shot. They tell you he went to the hospital and I [say], "Okay, did he die, what you want me to do, he will be all right." The family says that is fucked up. I ask why that is fucked up. He just got a .22 in the shoulder, why, because he was playing with a fucking gun. Sitting in the room playing with a fucking gun while you are high and he was shot. Well what do you want me to do about it? People [say] it is tragic. People are like, you got no heart.

Participants further explained their wives did not understand where they were at mentally and emotionally after their return from deployment. One participant stated:

> I remember telling my wife because we never got close like we were and we were having problems. I remember before I left I told her that I was broken and I did not feel what I felt before. It was not that I did not love her, I just didn't feel. I guess I kind of still don't, but I wouldn't ever tell her that because I don't want to break her heart; she doesn't understand, she wouldn't understand.

Another participant went into detail on this same topic: "My wife doesn't understand. She wants to know, but she will not understand. She [is] curious or wants to know everything, but she won't ever get it." This belief hinders an individual from being able to express the internal impact of deployment. This damages the relationship in that it diminishes the level of trust between partners, resulting in a loss of intimacy and communication.

A participant stated the importance of opening up to talk about the struggles of deployment and how his ability to do so allowed him to cope: "I was pretty fortunate that I was here when all that [happened], so I had the wife to talk to and all that kind of stuff." Another participant stated that his family views and treats him differently as a result of the deployments:

> It sucks to not be able to enjoy anything. I have to pretend to be happy. I have to pretend to laugh. So people do not sit there and bug me all the time. "Why aren't you happy, why aren't you laughing, why don't you go do this…" Last summer, my ex-wife took the kids to the water park I had to sit in the car most of the time because I could not deal with people at the water park. It is a big part because they are not being accepting [*sic*]. In addition, the family does not accept the fact that you know you. The looks they give you; they feel sorry for me.

Another participant discussed how his wife reacted to his behaviors after deployments:

> When I came home from deployment, they were building a new Lowe's and they were blowing up the rock around it with dynamite. I remember falling out of my bed one night by the sound of the

explosion, jumping on the ground, and my wife making fun of
me. That was really embarrassing.

Although his wife's response was a somewhat normal reaction to a person
unintentionally falling out of bed, the soldier misinterpreted the reaction
and internalized the response. Her lack of understanding about how to
respond pushed the participant further away. In another example of a
partner not understanding and responding in a maladaptive manner,
another participant stated:

> I was curled up around a bottle crying to my girlfriend to help
> me and she stood there screaming at me. Nobody wanted to help.
> I had to get away from it. I was unhappy walking into my own
> home. It is supposed to be a sanctuary.

One participant explained why he feels this reaction happens after
deployments:

> It is really, really hard to let your guard down and let somebody
> get close to you. Some of the most intimate relationships in my life
> was [sic] with my brothers. They could be just as easily ripped away
> from me as anything else could in the world. You never knew if
> you would see them day to day. So building that bond is difficult.
> You build it over months and days, and when you come home, it
> is a cluster when it comes to bonding with people or to building
> that connection. Whether friendship or romantic, it is difficult to
> connect to people.

This quote illustrates how soldiers often feel after deployment and why
then tend to shut out the important relationships in their lives. There is a
fear of getting close and allowing themselves to be vulnerable to the pain
of losing special relationships they have developed with fellow soldiers as
well as family members.

On the other hand, some participants spoke about supportive spouses
and how they handled situations following deployment:

> I was drinking. I wasn't able to control those feelings and it
> would end up with me crying and going off to be alone. My wife
> understood it and she would tell people, "Don't ask him about
> his deployment, just leave him alone about it and he will be fine."

One participant spoke in depth about how his relationship strengthened
after the deployment once he recognized he needed to open up:

For a while it caused issues in the relationship, but due to it, we are stronger. My wife and I are a lot stronger now. She has really helped a lot. We have become a lot stronger because of the SI attempt and the loss of the job. She has come to understand what I am going through and what I went through in the past. She did not really understand what I went through and what had happened. I did not really talk to her a lot about it. I have talked to her some about it now and she is trying to understand more about what I have been through."

Another participant discussed how he and his wife, who is also military, worked through the awkwardness of returning from deployments:

I came back and it was a lot different when we came back from the Afghanistan deployment where we came back together. Situation of your spouse already doing the things that go on in the house, I came back, and I am trying to fit in the situation again. Maybe more of a minor experience. There was a difference [and] it was hard and awkward to the daily stuff going on [*sic*]. I was trying to fit in and trying not to disrupt what she had going on. It was awkward. It was not what I remembered.

Better Off Being Alone

Participants described the property of Better Off Being Alone as being a "hermit." Participants also shared that they have had multiple relationships after deployments. One participant explained the feeling he had after seeing his family for the first time after the deployment:

My first deployment. When I got home my daughter was 3 and [deep breath] I was happy to see her and my wife but it was, like I knew, I do not know how to explain it. I just remember my wife getting into a big fight over me not being excited to see them. I was happy to be home, but I do not know… I think that was my first realization of being different, not being able to cope, or feeling like something is wrong with me. Not being excited to see my wife and my child.

Though the participants discussed this property as if they are better off being alone, there were indicators that the partners in the relationship were unable to communicate or work through the issues related to deployment. One participant shared:

> My wife and I separated Halloween and are going through divorce now. After my hospitalization…everything changed… So… She could not deal with it. My anxiety and all of that. While I was in the hospital, she decided to get a boyfriend. It is what it is.

Participants tended to minimize these feelings of loss and repressed the pain of losing a relationship. One participant went over the times he was married and then laid out all the injuries that he suffered while in the military:

> Married my first wife at 18, divorced at 21, remarried at 22, divorced in the military close to the end of carrier. The third I married on the day I retired and I am still waiting for the divorce now. There was a lot of turmoil and confusion, and now I am psychologically broken.

Another participant explained that he tried to talk to his wife, but in the process of trying to open up, pushed her away while trying to bring up the memories he was unwilling to share:

> My wife and I met after the deployment. Mom and sister say I am not the same person. I withdraw a little about me, how things happened. However, I never sat down and talked to them about it. My wife and I talked a little, but not [in] detail. There are certain things I have not told my wife about. She is always asking me what is going on. I won't tell her what I am thinking about it.

Push Away My Family

Participants described the property of Push Away My Family as something they must do "because of the way they see me now." This property relates to the participants' relationships with their children. One participant shared, "My children are scared of me and think I'm a monster now." Another participant described the shift in his family role from one of a protective nature to one that is closed off emotionally:

I put a lot of efforts into my family, my kids. I did not want them to have the stereotypical, crazy father, stuff like that. Especially with all the issues with my wife and my older daughter, I would lash out. They would push a button, which would go straight from 0-10 in 1.1 seconds. I tend to shut down or avoid it. You know what gets me upset? My wife wants to know, but doesn't want to know, but she will never understand what she would hear. She wants the knowledge, but will not understand the knowledge. It is something she would never get. It frustrates her, so when she gets to, she picks at it, picks at it, and picks at it. I am just like leave me alone. I will shut down. If she keeps on, I will just like yell or scream. She will ask, "What happened to you?" and I am like, "Leave it alone. I do not ask you what went on." Cause she had a bad childhood. In addition, it would be like me asking her [what] I want to know... Tell me everything... It's like, come on now. Why pick at the scab when it's not yours?

Another participant explained his inability to discuss his deployment with his family as opposed to discussing it with fellow soldiers:

You don't have to worry about judging the young soldiers; they do it themselves. It has been like that since I was in basic training. They were terrified, I was terrified, I didn't put it out there as much, but I think it helped them. In addition, it helped me, too... Yeah, it helped me. How I am and how I was—I do not know which is better. I do not feel as much, that I cannot be [*sic*], or maybe it has been so long ago that everybody has gotten use to how I am versus how I was. Maybe they just don't say anything to me about it anymore.

He elaborated on changes in his family's communication:

There was a time that my wife and my son and my daughter once talked about it, that I wasn't there—I wasn't home when I was home. They got used to it or I am back enough that, you know I am here, I am just not what I was. I used to be a patient person. Whatever I was doing, I was 150% there; now I am 90% there, which is better than I was. It is a little here and there. Being retired has helped.

One participant explained how the change in his duties from deployment to being a drill SGT [Sergeant] resulted in marital issues between him and his wife:

> My wife hit a rocky patch. A very rocky patch. I lost the stress of being a drill SGT [Sergeant], but I was under the stress that I might lose my wife of 12 to 13 years. That sent me in a tailspin. Everything started to come out then.

Overall, it appeared that the participants possessed the belief that their traumatic memories were unbearable, both for themselves and for others. In addition, participants were reluctant to share their traumatic memories in fear that the painful emotions associated with those memories would return. This fear caused the soldiers to avoid sharing their deployment experience with their family members.

Life Here is Petty

Participants described the property of Life Here is Petty as a result of deployment and the impact it had on their worldview. One of the participants stated, "After the things I have seen, the family will not understand this." One participant explained that following deployment, they noticed a change in the way they felt about the world around them as opposed to the world they saw while deployed:

> That's one of those things that I second guess, my interaction with people all the time. I really do not interact. I do not know what I should, how I should react or act with people. Lots of things people have as far as it being a big deal to them, I do not have or care about. I do not hold small talk conversations. I do not care. People want to tell me about new shoes coming out, I'm like, "I don't care."

Overall, participants reported a disruption in their ability to enjoy aspects of life that were important to them prior to deployment, as they had seen parts of life during deployment that one does not experience in daily life as a civilian.

Worry about Stupid Things When I Have Faced Death

Participants described the property of Worry about Stupid Things When I Have Faced Death as encompassing their feelings about how daily life unfolds after the profound experience of combat. One participant stated:

> I only see things in black or white. My wife has to deal with this on a day-to-day basis because I only see things on the logical side. Right or wrong, it is how to handle the situation logically. I don't do anything emotionally; it is all calculated.

Another participant elaborated on this point and how the pettiness of daily life tends to become aggravating:

> My wife will tell you that I am less tolerant of things. It is just that I put up with a lot of things back then that I am more likely to argue about. I think it is because when we have been on the edge for so long, you expect things to be treated with respect. And when you get home, you get things like, "Why didn't you take out the trash. Does that really matter?" It is one of her pet peeves with me, but to me, it is silly. It is like the microwave issue at home. I will push the 30-second button three times for a minute and a half, and my wife will ask why I am being lazy. To me it is no different—it is the same amount of buttons to push, but she will get upset about me not doing it that way. I think, "Does it affect you at all, I mean does it really affect you, no, then why are you complaining?"

This participant explained the rationale behind feeling that things are petty:

> Comes from experiencing life and death and this is trivial. Triviality does not matter, once you face life and death, the trivialities for me are just background noise. It just doesn't matter to me. If I decide I am going to put on a sock, then a shoe, rather than two socks then two shoes, what difference does it make to somebody else? The only person it should make a difference to is me. It does not affect you... Why do you care? Why are you bothering me with your trivia when it does not matter in the big scheme of things? The big scheme of things is life and death and surviving.

Summary

Relationships are a balancing act for soldiers following deployment. Soldiers tend to view their spouse as a threat to their survival while they are deployed due to the distraction it presents in their ability to stay focused during missions. However, the healthy relationship that is beginning to have problems can cause the soldier to bring up issues related to the deployment. As we understand the complexity of the relationship between the deployable soldier and the soldiers who have returned from deployments, there is an expectation that the family members will support them upon their return and throughout their retirement. However, it is apparent that the soldiers have a complex response in that they do not want to open up emotionally to their family in fear that they will be unable to face the memory and emotional response to the memory. The level of fear, triumph, and rage that is experienced is overwhelming and difficult to manage alongside the complexity of the memories of deployment, as well as the self-concepts that have been interwoven into the beliefs of the self.

Category 6: Not Heard

All participants described feeling Not Heard by their commands, therapists, doctors, and/or families. This category consists of the following properties: Army and Veteran Association (VA) Therapists are not Listening; Therapist Sticks to Structured Manual Therapy; Therapist and Family Can't Handle It; Only Understood by Other Military People Who Have Deployed; and Only Understood by People in the Same MOS.

Army and VA Therapists Are not Listening

One consistent theme in the interviews was that participants felt that their Army and VA therapists were not listening to them. Participants stated: "They don't get it" and "One of my therapists would whip out a coping skill to do whenever I brought the trauma up, how is that supposed to help?" The experience of feeling shut down when they finally decided to speak up about their experiences while deployed only reinforced the feeling of not being heard and kept them from fully sharing the memory. One participant stated, "I had multiple therapists in the time I was in behavioral health. Each time I opened up, it was to a new person who I had to explain the whole thing to again, and they don't care." The following is another example of this phenomenon:

Bobbie, this has been the most therapeutic thing I have done since I got home. When I sat down to talk to therapists in the past, it has always been like they stop me and hit on the one thing and don't let me go any further. It's frustrating because there is a revolving door of therapists at the VA. Every new therapist I had to retell the story to while I was there. It would just anger me. It was like, just read the fucking case before I walk in. It was terrible, too, with the psychiatrist because they did the same with the meds. As far as the therapist aspect, no one ever just let me talk, there was always a stopping point and it was like, huh, there it is, even if I wasn't done. This has been the most therapeutic for me so far. This has been pretty great and I'm glad I took part in this.

Another participant explained the feeling of being in a VA group setting, stating that being placed in groups with soldiers from different branches of the military caused them to feel misunderstood by the group members. Although this could fall in the property of Only Being Understood by the Same MOS (Military Occupational Specialty), it also describes this participant's VA group experience:

To be able to talk to somebody who has been there might help, but they have those wonderful VA support groups [sarcasm]. I tried that and a lot of these are guys, I'm thinking, are going to be in combat support groups. I get there and I get a bunch of National Guard guys that never deployed and a bunch of Airforce. It was like, really…you never done anything, how am I going to talk to these guys and relate? I remember talking about one circumstance and this one guy said, "That is fucking crazy." I was like, "See, that was a normal day for me and that is why I don't come to these things." I was like, "I came here to get help and you came to feel like you're war heroes." If they actually put combat soldiers in with combat soldiers that would be alright. It is so hard to filter and screen that. It is sad.

Therapist Sticks to Structured Manual Therapy

Participants discussed the feeling of the therapist not caring, which relates to the property of Therapist Sticks to Structured Manual Therapy. One participant shared, "I've done EMDR and CPT, but it always feels like they just don't want to hear your stories." The experience of taking the step to open up is put on a manualized procedure format, which participants felt prevented them from fully opening up. The following is an example of this phenomenon: "Just as I start to feel comfortable, I am asked to take out an ABC log and work it out on paper. I even go to a follow-up group and we all have to pull out the ABC log to work on." Another participant expressed a need to be heard without interruption: "I feel like I am only understood by other military people who have deployed, only understood by people in the same MOS, like I don't want to open up to therapist who can't handle hearing trauma." This statement illustrates the difficulty some participants had in believing a therapist can work with the experiences they have had during deployments.

Therapist and Family Can't Handle Real Trauma Stories

One theme observed throughout the participants' stories was that of Therapist and Family Can't Handle Real Trauma Stories. One participant stated, "I can't tell my wife what I did and what I saw, she can't handle it," while another shared, "My therapist said she had a nightmare about what I told her." These reactions to the participants sharing their stories caused them to feel as if they are unable to open up to the people in their lives in whom they should be able to confide, which can ultimately result in them closing themselves off to these relationships. One participant described an attempt to open up to a therapist which resulted in his being misunderstood:

> I started doing things that took me out of my comfort zone. I would go to McDonalds and sit with my back to a door, or something that posed a threat. I had to learn how to get comfortable. I had a therapist once tell me, "Don't you think they just might want a Big Mac or something?" I told him, "At the time, I don't care

what they want. They could be a threat and if they are a threat, well then…even seeing things on the news, the world is not a good place."

This is an example of the therapist not fully understanding the soldier's state of mind as he shares his experiences after deployment. Participants reported that therapists have tried to push them into believing they are safe, after they have been living in combat and facing death on a daily basis. This experience of the therapist not understanding or pushing the soldier to a place he is not emotionally ready to go can cause the soldier to stop opening up about his experience. The following statement illustrates this phenomenon:

Soldiers don't associate with civilians because it is a different lifestyle. It is even harder when you can't find that common ground. There has to be therapists that have dealt with things like being robbed at gunpoint, or some sort of PTSD to relate to what that soldier is going through.

Some of the participants made statements regarding how therapists can gain a more thorough understanding of their experience. One participant stated:

I think every therapist should go on the website "I Was There" to understand what the soldiers are going through. Every time I watch the new films, I am in tears because I can associate with what they are going through.

Several participants stated that when they feel unable to fully share a memory, they are impacted those who cannot hear their story. One participant stated, "My wife doesn't want to hear this," while another remarked, "I start to tell them what happened, but they don't get it." The participants explained how they felt ready to share their story, but the individuals to whom they spoke expressed that they did not want to, or were unable to, listen or understand. This caused the participants to stop talking about the memory, hindering their ability to fully open up about their experience. The following quotes provide an example of this phenomenon: "Nobody wants to hear about how I saw a man decapitated"; "I need to talk about how I walked up on dead body parts, but who can hear that?"; and "If I talk about it then they will react like I am crazy." Compounding this belief of not feeling heard is the belief that talking about it will make things worse or cause it to be relived. One participant shared:

> A lot of us keep a lot of stuff compartmentalized and locked away. We don't like to talk about a lot of stuff locked up and tucked away. That is the best way, unfortunately, for me to deal with it. At least for me, I have found that over years of going to counseling, I am constantly talking about it and it made my nightmares worse. It made things manifest subconsciously, without being able to have any control over it. So I found, the less I talk about it, the better off I am emotionally and mentally.

This thinking can cause a block in the therapeutic process as well as in relationships, where soldiers feel it is better to repress the memory rather than open up about it.

Only Understood by Other Military Persons Who Have Been Deployed

The feeling of being unable to fully open up to other people falls under the category of "Only Understood by Other Military People Who Have Been Deployed." This category expresses the feeling of being understood only by those who have had the same experiences. However, it is a balancing act of sorts, as not enough sharing of mutual experiences can be as bad as too much sharing. "No offense, but you can't understand what I saw." "I can tell you, but you're not going to understand this." These statements express the participants' feeling that other soldiers who have deployed can understand them and that I, as the interviewer, will not understand the full extent of what they are trying to convey. They explained that only deployment and being in these conditions will help somebody to understand what it was like to deploy. One participant stated, "We all experienced the same things," while another reported, "Everyone heard IED and mortars every day." One of the higher ranked participants stated:

> These guys work very hard at physical therapy and rehabilitation to get back to where they were before. It is their own self-image and their peers' view of them that they are trying to repair, because the most important opinion in their lives is their buddies they have

been in combat with. When you become broke, you are no longer mission capable; you are no longer a part of the team any more, and you feel like you are letting buddies down. So you strive to get back to that point.

This viewpoint is helpful in understanding the bond that the soldiers form while deployed and how this impacts the self-ideals that the soldiers have developed. This is explained further in the following statement:

Soldiers will not respect a senior leader, who cannot lead. I was not allowed to go on runs with them, so I took the guys on profile and did Physical Training (PT) with them and exhausted them. They did not want to do PT with me anymore. I violated it because I was bound and determined to be a leader. When that final straw hit it was very hard.

However, portions of some interviews described how talking with other soldiers about deployments caused a reaction they either were not ready for or did not want.

I had to separate myself from them a little bit. I still call him on the phone and check on him every now and then, but he worries me. If I go out there and we will spend the day talking about all of his problems and all of his issues, then I'm going to be able to relate to him. As I relate to his issues, it also opens up that box of stuff that I have already put away, and then I go into a really dark place.

Conversely, participants also explained that there is a need for soldiers to have been in the same MOS to understand each other's experience. The data also point to an important dimension of feeling broken, in that a central part of the experience is feeling separated from the group of fellow combatants, spouses, and family.

Only Understood by People in the Same MOS

Participants reported that they only felt understood by other military people who have deployed and that this experience deepened if the soldiers they talked to were in the same MOS. One participant stated, "I can't talk to FOBITS, they don't get it," while another shared, "It really helps to talk to the guys I deployed with." Another participant stated, "There is one guy who deployed with me who I talk to, because he saw the same things." The soldiers have a need to open up with others like them in order to share a deeper experience of their deployments. One participant stated, "There is a difference in talking to people you deployed with and people who you did not," while another confessed, "I can't show my feelings to the guys, they need to see that I am strong to keep them strong." It appears that even the rank of the individual changes according to whether or not he is able to open up and talk about the events he has seen.

There appears to be a trust issue that is felt amongst soldiers, which feeds this belief that they can only talk to other soldiers. One participant stated, "Soldiers trust other soldiers who have been in the same experience as they have. They don't necessarily trust those who have not been in the same experience as them." In this feeling of trust, only those who have experienced the same type of deployments can relate. The following participant quote is an example of this phenomenon:

> It is very, very exhausting for me. Usually after I do that for five days, I go home and sleep for about 14 hours. It's helping others while I am trying to curb my own emotions. When I am hearing other people talk, I try not to judge them and their experiences. Being a combat vet who works with other combat vets, I can be very judgmental, but I don't ever let people know that. My combat experience may be different from somebody else's experience. I might not consider theirs combat. There might be thoughts like, "So what a bomb blew up near you, you weren't hurt, you never fired your weapon, I don't understand why this is hurting you so bad nobody got hurt?" Whereas I had multiple engagements up close with the enemy, so when I am doing these I really have to put my judgmental part aside and help them with their PTSD, so when this is over I am really exhausted. I don't ever let them know that, but in my head I am thinking, shut up.

Although participants reported that they judged soldiers in a different MOS as having different experiences than they did during combat, they attempted to empathize with the other soldiers' experiences and appeared to have an internal dialog around their feeling that it was wrong to judge the other soldiers. The following participant quote illustrates this phenomenon:

> Maybe my empathy is broken for some people, too. People that have done the same thing I do, I truly have empathy for, and some people I come across, we will say their combat experience that they got PTSD from. I am like, "What was so bad about that, you didn't get hurt, nobody got hurt."

Several participants demonstrated reactions that showed a positive experience of opening up to the soldiers with whom they deployed. One of these responses was very clear:

> Since I got out, I have had my dog tags hanging on the review mirror of my truck as a reminder of everything that I love, the country, the Army, my friends. Where I am now and where I will be, all because of the things I learn from serving my country, meeting those people and the experiences that I have had. Everything that happened to me that was emotional it has been a blessing for me.

Many of the participants discussed the importance of the friendships they developed with other soldiers while they were deployed and explained why these relationships were so important. The following participant quote illustrates this phenomenon:

> The friends I had over, they talk about the loss of their friends that died. You talk about how hard it was and how bad it pisses you off that you're over there helping them and they do something like this. It became more about kissing babies and shaking hands and still all the dumb crap happening. You talk about how you want to be one to the guys to take care of the guys that did this to them, but then you talk about the funny things and the good stuff and the good times.

One participant explained how the impact of their friendship caused the soldiers to listen to each other, but that they did not have much time to process due to the combat situation. However, they attempted to process their feelings once they returned from deployment or when they had free time. The following illustrates this phenomenon:

> We still have a job to do. You talk about them, you listen to the other brothers that are talking about them crying and just trying to get through this stuff. For me it just makes you do the best that you can, so everybody else gets to come home.

The soldier further explained the reason behind the bond: "It makes you think about regardless how big or small and how important your job was it had to be done to insure the safety of everybody else."

This participant went on to state that the memories of that which had occurred during his deployment had helped him to grow as a person. Another participant discussed the experience of self-growth and how it enabled him to help those with whom he was deployed.

> That was the thing in my personal life that assisted me on the emotional part, to help look for the positives and not continue talking about all the soldiers we lost. Some of them I was close to that I looked up to, because they were senior leaders and it affected me to the point that I had my own personal issues.

Camaraderie was mentioned as an important factor in allowing soldiers to confront the issues they face while deployed, as well as upon their return from deployment. One participant explained the difference between the two units he worked with in the following quote:

> Where I am at in the military going from the one unit to the one I am in now… There was teamwork, camaraderie, but because of the bond you went through we would BS together, and where I am now everyone is out for themselves they will trample you to get ahead. It is cutthroat. There is no team.

The bond between the soldiers that deploy together is strong enough that they can share an understanding without the need for words. This helps soldiers process their experiences with others who know what they are going through. The following illustrates this phenomenon:

> I talked about it with my roommate during deployment, and we are still pretty close. He was just kind of there, but not a "we need to talk" kind of there. He would just come and sit beside me and be like, "Hey I got you." Just the peace of it being quiet…

Summary

Not Heard is a profound category that encompasses the following properties: Army and Veteran Association (VA) Therapists are not Listening, Therapist Sticks to Structured Manual Therapy, Therapist and Family Can't Handle It, Only Understood by Other Military People Who Have Deployed, and Only Understood by People in the Same MOS. Each of the properties within this category triggered raw emotions that elevated the emotional response to the questions asked in the interviews. As the participants discussed the properties, expressions of anger and aggression penetrated the issues and were complicated by the participants' symptoms following deployment. When dealing with such raw feelings, it is human nature for individuals to feel an acute need for others to get it just right, or right enough. The participants described feeling as if they are not heard or understood and are confused about why they are not being helped. This continues to complicate the successful processing needed to move on.

FINDINGS AND IMPLICATIONS

The following chapter outlines and discusses the five findings. The implications of each finding will then be discussed, followed by limitations of the study, clinical implications, and implications for future research.

Brief Description of Findings

Finding 1: Numbness results in a withdrawal from relationships and social engagement.

Ultimately, the impact of the complex experiences of war on the self is a powerful phenomenon that was found in all categories of the study. Numbness was described throughout the interviews, with the participants giving insight into how the deployments caused a mental and emotional shut down and/or multiple separations within the self. The participants described this phenomenon as a disabling component which caused their self to change in such a way that their families took notice. They also described their own experience of the change across their social environment and their internalization of a radically new self-perception.

Finding 2: Experiencing death, witnessing death or injuries of people close to them, and realizing that they could get killed at any time results in lasting psychological changes.

The participants described a shift in the way they experienced the harsh reality of death. They moved from a realization that death can occur to the recognition that they are going to die. This realization of the possibility of death was described in two ways: (a) they try to protect themselves and everyone around them and (b) they do not care as they are going to die by their own hands. This psychological shift resulted in risk-taking behavior and a lack of caution.

Finding 3: Idealization of command is promoted and drilled into soldiers during training.

Idealization in classical Kohutian theory states that individuals need to feel close to someone bigger, wiser, and more competent who promotes a sense of security and ability. Idealization of command is destined to be ruptured during the chaos of war due to variability in command skill and experience, and any preexisting deficits in idealization are bound to be repeated in the unpredictable nature of war. However, while this is an important aspect, soldiers repeatedly emphasized that this was not the cause of feeling broken.

Finding 4: Survival guilt is bad news.

The participants described an ongoing guilt over their survival, and ongoing idealization of the deceased, and an identification with the deceased.

Finding 5: Physically broken, mentally broken, and emotionally broken.

Participants stated that feeling broken is comprised of three aspects: physically broken, mentally broken, and emotionally broken. These were further explained as a confluence of events, where experiences of death and disappointment come together and alter their perception of who they are.

Theoretical Implications

Finding 1: Numbness results in a withdrawal from relationships and social engagement.

The numbness that participants described provided insight into the withdrawal and self-protection that is needed to withstand the injuries they endured in combat and upon return from combat to their "normal" state of life. These efforts at self-protection also often resulted in interpersonal problems. All emotions are potentially threatening, for the fear of what else they may feel.

Freud (1920) explained that the stimulus barrier has been breached by the external stimuli, causing the protective shield to block dangers that are perceived to cause damage. This stimulus barrier is ruptured in deployment and participants explained how they have numbed themselves to keep from feeling any more pain. This was described by Freud as the process of,

> reception of certain specific effects of stimulation, but which also include special arrangements for further protection against excessive amounts of stimulation and for excluding unsuitable kinds of stimuli. It is characteristic of them that they deal only with very small quantities. (p. 27)

The participants explained that this theory describes the way they took in the experience of war and the way in which their feelings began to numb as they return home. The amount of stimuli experienced overwhelmed their ability to process and work through emotions related to the stimuli. The participants explained that once they returned home, they shut down this ability due to being overwhelmed by the emotions that have flooded them throughout their deployments. Therefore, the participants explained the process of their withdrawal from the social environment to maintain any further damage to themselves.

Kardiner (1941) explained that traumatic neurosis consists of a fixation phenomenon accompanied by a repetitive process with a group of secondary defense mechanisms. The defense mechanism that the participants described was identified as numbing themselves. This process blocks the unpleasant feelings from flooding them when they are triggered. Kardiner further explained that exposure creates events which are difficult to escape and activates disorganization of the ego (Kardiner, 1941). The participants experienced a change in how they react to uncomfortable feelings and memories.

Kardiner (1941) stated that "activity of war represents a stripping of refinements of social organization with effect of releasing anxiety in the form of fear." This explanation provides insight into why the participants numbed their experiences of fear during deployment and why they continued to do so after returning home. The feeling of fear counters who they believe they are as well as who they feel they should be as a man, father, husband, son, and friend. This causes the participants to numb their feelings to prevent any further breakdown in the face of the anxiety and fears they have endured in war, as well as perceived danger in their normal environments at home.

Ornstein (1994) described how one processes the impact a traumatic memory has on the psyche. She explained that an individual integrates the traumatic memory into the psyche and encounters an obstacle due to the conflict built into the memory. The memory is feared because of its potential to bring back the traumatic experience (Ornstein, 1994). Participants explained this as part of the numbing which keeps the memories, as well as the accompanying emotions, from returning. The participants also expressed their fear that the emotional flood would also impact their relationships with family and friends.

Ornstein (1994) explained that Integration depends on the resolution of this dialog of the memory to be discussed. She further stated that empathy allows for the difficult psychological task to take place, which explains why the participants reported that they could only talk to their buddies because they are the only ones who understand.

Ornstein (1994) explained Disavowal as a mental mechanism that helps to alter a state of consciousness. This creates a state of mind that numbs affect to make survival of a traumatic experience possible. This process of Disavowal was created by the participants to split off the affect to keep themselves safe from the affect that accompanies the memory of the deployments. The act of numbing was created to avoid any breach of this memory, in order to prevent themselves from feeling the way they did in the deployment or in the memory of the deployment. Ornstein expounded that disavowal is a defense; it splits reality while allowing one to wish for a situation to exist. Numbness serves to protect soldiers from the feelings they get in touch with in social situations and family situations, such as feeling damaged, different, not like familiar people, and, as some participants stated, like a "killer."

Finding 2: Experiencing death, witnessing death or injuries of people close to them, and realizing that they could get killed at any time results in lasting psychological changes.

While Freud (1920) referred to "railway collisions and other near death experiences," he went on to emphasize "concussive events" and the impact of "near death" which receded into the background of trauma theory. Stolorow (2007) began to address the idea of "near death" using Heidegger and his concept of the authenticity of death. He looked at the way death is understood by the individual and explained how death becomes a possibility in the face of trauma. He stated that death has a potential and certainty. He also explained that anticipating the unknown certainty of death opens up a constant threat (Stollorow, 2007, p. 375).

This threat of death and fear of its permanency caused the soldiers to look toward death in a different way than they did prior to facing their own death, a fellow soldier's death, or even their enemy's death. Stollorow (2007) further explained that the greater the possibility of death, the more deeply this will impact the person facing death (Stollorow, 2007, p. 374). The participants explained that the closer they were to the combat, the more real it became to them. They made statements such as, "Oh shit, this is really happening." The reality of facing death is often not fully grasped in training and is not truly felt until in the middle of a war zone. In this situation, soldiers are facing their own death, which causes them to start focusing on staying alive. Staying alive includes keeping their buddies alive as well. The permanency of death is not reality until they are in the midst of this happening. Stollorow stated that "death already belongs to our existence." However, people tend to want to remove themselves from this reality. The participants recalled that they always thought they would come back and would bring their buddies back alive. While this allows them to distance themselves from the reality of death, it also sets themselves up for failure, as death is a part of our existence and our reality.

Freud (1919) described war neurosis as a conflict in the ego. Freud stated that the conflict lies in the peaceful ego that the participants described as their old self which they cannot get back. According to Freud, a new ego develops during war time (p. 208). The participants explained that the old self, which Freud referred to as the peace-ego, becomes acute once it realizes the danger in the face and realization of the possibility of death (Freud, 1919, p. 208). The participants also discussed what Freud described as taking flight into the traumatic neurosis to defend itself from a new ego. The participants expressed that the "new ego" they observed was frightening and misunderstood by themselves and the people within their personal lives. This new ego that the participants experienced was foreign and was exposed to realities such as death, a level of aggression that is foreign, and an often deep desire to retaliate for friends killed in battle. This intensity of feelings and fantasies are not understood by their old civilian ego, which at times causes confusion and even horror when the self observes the degree of aggressive fantasies.

Finding 3: Idealization of command is promoted and drilled into soldiers during training.

Fairbairn (1952) promoted the theoretical idea that command becomes a bad object in the process of combat. He explained that the object would be rejected if it could be the bad object and is forced upon the individual; in addition, it can be resisted because of the power it holds over the individual (Fairbairn, 1952). At this point, the person is forced to internalize the bad object, the command, in an effort to control confusing feelings and alterations in the repressive forces of good objects (Fairbairn, 1952). The participants related the need for the command, regardless of whether they are good or bad, as Fairbairn also explained. Participants explained that without leadership, there is a risk of facing more dangers, and more risks are taken. This also illustrates the not always recognized differences between actual and perceived threats. Therefore, the participants described a process of needing the command to be a good object even through the command is a bad object. They turned and looked toward the command for their own safety and the safety of their fellow soldiers, as they were going into combat facing the possibility of death or severe injury. If they faced this reality of death with a realization that the command is a bad object, they may have entered into a dangerous situation with a mindset that increases the risk of death.

Kardiner (1941) stated that it is important for the soldier to identify his self with the cause only because it enables him to be involved. The participants spoke to the fact that they were unable to identify with the cause of the war when the command failed to explain the mission well. They were aware of the direct mission of the task at hand, but not of the overall political mission as to why they were there in the first place. This caused a withdrawal from the command and separation from the idealization of the command. When the soldier has identified with the cause and the leaders and has ties with the group, the soldier is better able to process the anxiety caused by the war situation (Kardiner, 1941). Participants explained that if the command is leading them, they will fight for that command with no questions asked. However, when the safety and security of that command is not present, the participants become overwhelmed by vulnerability.

Kohut (1971) stated that people seek out others who are more powerful and calm. This is promoted in training and enhanced, but invariably disrupted. Participants explained that at times they could "work through" the disruption, while other soldiers remained in a disrupted state. The more they are able to comfortably idealize their commanders, the stronger and more confident they feel in the act of combat. When the powerful and calm approach is lacking and they view the command as questioning the mission and as unsure of themselves, the participants stated that disruption and fear floods them. This is the point at which the participants begin to take things in their own hands. They blame themselves for their unpreparedness when it is actually the command which is to blame. When the soldier does not feel lead, they will walk into the danger blinded. However, when they have idealized the command, they will walk in feeling more prepared and ready to follow, which creates a feeling of cohesion among the unit.

Finding 4: Survival guilt is bad news.

The participants described an ongoing guilt over survival, an ongoing idealization of the deceased, and an identification with the deceased.

Freud (1913, 1917) first coined the term "survivor guilt" and hypothesized that the nature of survivor guilt is in the doubt felt towards the deceased. Freud (1913) explained doubt as the individual also experiencing ambivalence or aggression towards the deceased. He explained that there is a conflict between the emotions toward the deceased loved one, which causes this doubt to occur (Freud, 1913). The participants expressed the complexity of their feelings toward the lost or injured soldier and discussed the confusion felt over the feelings of guilt and shame they had amidst their responses and thoughts toward them. Details were provided that gave insight into the thoughts of gratitude that they themselves did not die, but feelings of shame and guilt for having this thought.

Freud (1915) was attentive to the complex and psychological impacts of war on both soldiers and civilians. The participants talked repeatedly about the bonds that form during combat. Freud did not address the role of survival pacts and the role pledges of mutual survival play in the development of survivor guilt. The participants related how bonds deepened while working together as a team to save another's life and the intense experience of their life being saved by the actions of a fellow soldier, which becomes a complex psychological event. Another layer that deepens this psychological process is when the soldier is unable to save their fellow soldier or even when they are unable to save a civilian man, woman, or child during their mission. This results in a profound sense of defeat, which in turn causes the second guessing and guilt to occur. Participants discussed this reaction as they processed the emotions felt when they were unable to be there when one of their friends died, when they should have been on the deployment rather than one of their fellow soldiers, or when they were unable to save the baby they held in their arms. These incidents internalize and create a complex emotional response, thereby creating confusion and often unrelenting self-blame.

Niederland (1968) conferred the consequences of Survival Guilt. He explained that Survivor Syndrome has three components: Reactive Depression, Anxiety Syndrome, and Survival Guilt (Niederland, 1968). The participants stated that they experienced Reactive Depression after returning from deployment. They discussed the decline in their relationships and the withdrawal from their social environment. Anxiety Syndrome was discussed as occurring around the time they began to think about the deceased and began having thoughts about how it should have been them. This was also described as leading into anger and/or drinking in order to not feel the anxiety and/or rage, or to prevent them from turning on themselves. The Survival Guilt symptom is one that the participants declined to discuss in depth. They would typically begin to experience depression and anxiety as they talked through these questions and then find a way to readjust themselves to be able to continue. This aspect of Survival Guilt is profound and debilitating as they are flooded with intense emotions. Niederland (1968) explained that Survival Guilt can lead to two distinct components: the Depressive Component (depression, apathy, seclusion) and the Persecutory Component (fear, vigilance, paranoid reactions). Shelby (1990) stated:

> Survivor guilt appears to be particularly intense when a mutual survival pact has been made. Along with relief of being alive (however brief or unconscious) the survivor may be left with a profound sense of having failed a sworn oath.

Participants discussed feeling a strong responsibility to bring back their fellow soldiers. The participants who had higher ranks explained this as a responsibility to their fellow soldiers' families and to their units. They have a sense of loyalty that is considered broken when they are unable to bring back all members of their unit and then blame themselves for the incident that caused the death to occur. The interviews indicated multiple layers of "survival pacts": between individuals, between command and their lower ranking troops and their families, and between command and other commanders. Clearly, some of these pledges to "get each other out alive" were spoken, while others were imagined. Regardless of their exact nature, the psychological consequences can be profound and challenging for the surviving soldiers to resolve.

Finding 5: Physically broken, mentally broken, and emotionally broken.

The confluence of events, experiences of death, disfiguring injuries, and disappointment all came together for the men in this study. These profound experiences changed who they knew themselves to be prior to deployment. The participants made statements referring to the feeling of not being able to get back who they were before the experience of the war. "I am broken" consists of a desperate need to get back who they were, but all of these factors stand in the way.

Fairbairn (1952) explained that preventing the psychological neurosis of war is dependent upon the command remaining a good object. He explained that only under successful leadership will the soldier be able to depend upon their command. If the command fails, then they turn into the bad object, leaving the soldier to interlay this threat and hold the bad object as their own failure (Fairbairn, 1952).

Freud (1919) stated:

> The cause of all war neuroses was an unconscious inclination in the soldier to withdraw from the demands, dangerous or outrageous to his feelings, made upon him by active service. Fear of losing his own life, opposition to the command to kill other people, rebellion against the ruthless suppression of his own personality by his superiors—these were the most important. (p. 211)

This describes what the participants explained as being physical, mental, and emotionally broken. The soldiers defined being physically broken as a change in their physical state—being unable to physically do what they did before. They defined being mentally broken as being unable to process or function in memory or mental tasks; this also encompasses psychological functioning. They defined being emotionally broken in relationship to how they handled life after deployment. They shared that they have shut down and are unable feel things like they did before deployment. They clearly stated that this feeling of being emotionally broken is not PTSD; rather, it is the fear of feeling that they do not know what will happen if they allow themselves to feel again. This description goes beyond the *DSM-IV* and *DSM-5*'s definitions of PTSD in that the other symptoms are not described. The "numbness" that they feel is directly related to the fear of an overwhelming catharsis of their emotions. They explained that this results in the "shutdown" of emotions to repress and avoid a folding of affect.

A central disagreement in Freud's and Fairbairn's theories of war trauma is that Freud's focus was on a discrete event that ruptures the "stimulus barrier" and Fairbairn's emphasis was on a series of separations from "good objects" that have a repressive force on "bad objects."

As the analysis of the data was provided by the participants, the idea of being broken as the result of a discrete event was present. However, as the participants talked, it became obvious that it was not one individual event which contributed to the feeling of being broken, but rather an overall exposure to the multiple deployments and events which took place. Soldiers are repeatedly exposed to events that are impossible to integrate. This combined with disappointment in command and the failure to live up to a survival pact may result in behavioral problems or feelings of defeat, shame, and fear.

Towards a Theory of "Feeling Broken"

The purpose of this study was to explore through the analysis of in-depth interviews the phenomenon of feeling broken. The goal of grounded theory is to develop a theory about a particular experience among groups of individuals encountering similar phenomena. As such, it is a substantive theory and not a formal theory that applies to a wide range of people and situations.

The participants explained that there are many aspects which contribute to feeling broken. They stated that it is not simply attributed to one event which occurred. The following progression was apparent across the 15 participants' accounts of the impacts of their deployments and their path to being broken.

First, they See Death and Horrific Injuries or Face Their Own Death. This phase seems to be a process that triggers deeper meanings that are difficult to integrate. This process also causes unresolved feelings toward the person who died or who was injured, and impacts soldiers' ability to comprehend their own reality of death and their relief at being alive.

The second phase is Do Not Care if They Live or Die. This phase seems to transpire once the soldiers have fully accepted the reality that they could die at any moment. This is not expressed as suicidality. Rather, it is a form of acceptance that they are going to die. This seems to come after they have arrived at the war zone and have had a taste that war brings death. The soldiers are not prepared for the reality of war until they have seen death in the many forms that they are exposed to in a third world country that has many different beliefs about death.

The third phase is Risk Taking or Taking Things in Their Own Hands. The participants discussed their lack of faith in the command and their attempts to integrate the death they have experienced at this point. The participants explained that they began to take risks and do what they needed to do to protect their fellow soldiers, and that they would run into the face of danger to keep a person alive. However, what we are seeing here is a part of the psyche that is trying to protect itself from seeing more death. The psyche at this point is overwhelmed when these types of risks are being taken. The soldiers are protecting others by putting their own lives in danger, but in a sense, they are also saving themselves from the collapse of their own psyche.

The fourth phase is the Dissolve of Relationships. This is seen in the interaction with command during the deployments. The participants discussed the faith they placed in the leadership when they first deployed. As they experienced increased loss of injured soldiers and more death, they began to distance themselves from this relationship due to not trusting the leadership to keep them alive and safe. This distrust ultimately transferred over to their relationships once they returned home to their families. They experienced a successful way to handle loss and death while deployed by repressing their emotions, or, as the participants described it, "turning it off." This defense was successful, but also resulted in a disconnect from their families and friends, ultimately destroying their personal relationships. The disconnect from family may have begun prior to deployment or during deployment, but the ultimate impact was not felt until they returned from deployment and engaged in day-to-day interactions with family and friends.

The fifth phase is Mind Changes. This phase can start while deployed, but was mostly discussed within the context of their return. The participants explained a process of no longer knowing who they are, as well as the experience of their families no longer knowing who they are. This leads the soldiers into thinking that they no longer know what to do with all of the changes they have gone through, resulting in a feeling of hopelessness and despair. All of these phases together result in the soldier feeling broken. This is a dramatic shift from being at the top of their game, to being broken and feeling broken. This implies that it is necessary for the friends and family of soldiers to realize that the soldiers need time to regain their awareness of who they are and to recognize themselves again.

Clinical Implications and Future Research

Clinical Implications

Based on the results of this study, the clinical approach to working with clients who have identified themselves as "broken," or who have deployed and experienced trauma, may need to be approached differently from how the majority of trauma treatments indicate. The data indicate that the participants do not consider "broken" to be the same as PTSD. Therefore, it is important to recognize that the current modality treatments ask therapists to single out discrete events and focus on one event only, thereby deterring clients from working on the environmental chaos that impacts the ways in which they internalize the trauma, their self-ideals, and the way they experience the world.

The participants indicated that the idea of focusing merely on a discrete event is complicated because the problem is multifaceted. Techniques such as Eye Movement Desensitization Reprocessing (EMDR), Cognitive Processing Therapy (CPT), and Prolonged Exposure Therapy (PET) are all beneficial in focusing on the discrete event. However, the study data indicate that further assistance from the therapist is needed to allow the soldier to open up and be allowed to process the ways in which the discrete event has impacted other parts of his or her life, such as family, spouse, friendships, and command. The disruptions in these relationships have profound implications. Multiple participants stated that they used the above mentioned modality and were unable to continue therapy; as a result, their lives collapsed in the area of their relationships.

Relationships play a significant role in maintaining latent or not fully conscious content. When therapists focus solely on the discrete event, they are working on the manifest content. This creates a conflict in the relationship problems that the solider is experiencing. The soldier is unable to look at how the discrete event played a part in the disruption in the relationship. The disruptions stem from separation and an inability to open up to one's family or spouse about the experience of deployments. The soldier's ability to open up to his or her family or spouse about the death he or she faced and how he or she is internalizing the loss of fellow soldiers or his or her own injuries provides needed support and strengthens relationships. It also helps to establish a feeling of wholeness and maintains the soldier's bond with family and spouse as opposed to separation and isolation. The importance of focusing on the disruption in the family or spousal relationship can help to improve the support system and self-ideal found through the family and spouse. As the therapist focuses on the impact over all deployments, or the impact of the self-identification of being broken, the soldier has the opportunity to discuss the multifaceted components of the self-ideal and to process the effects that deployment has had on his or her life.

Along with the disruption in the family or spousal relationship, the focus on the relationship with the command needs to be addressed. This relationship has a significant impact on the way in which the soldier processes the injuries and deaths of fellow soldiers and how the mission was approached. The data indicate that soldiers have difficulty placing the blame on the command; however, they have trust in the decisions and will follow the orders they are given. This disruption of questioning the leadership causes an internal process in which they question themselves and take the blame for the incident. This component needs to be processed to work through the complexity of the relationship with their command.

Processing through the various parts of the soldier's life which have been impacted by deployment during the therapeutic process would benefit the soldier by allowing him or her to find ways to open up to his or her intimate partner about the emotional impact the discrete event had on his or her life. This discrete event, however, may actually encompass more than one event. The study data echo controversies in the war trauma literature involving the tension between events, the separation between family, and increased dependence on command and comrades in arms.

In addition to the discrete event encompassing more than one event, it may involve survivor guilt as well. As therapists approach this unfamiliar experience with the soldier, they need to be aware that this is a very delicate matter which is extremely hard for the soldier to work through. The participants expressed their difficulty in verbalizing their emotions surrounding one area in particular, that of death. Death is difficult to comprehend and impacts individuals differently. There are multiple approaches that look at how to process bereavement and feelings of loss, guilt, and shame. However, the participants struggle to use these models due to the level of pain they feel and the meaning that the death has on who that person was as well as how it impacts how they have taken this person in as a self-ideal. Again, the findings echo the complexity of survivor guilt as explicated in the literature on survivor guilt.

As the individual brings forth the disruptions in relationships, the command disruptions are difficult to process. The participants explained that they do not blame their command, but that part of them holds the command responsible and feels the need to maintain the ideals for that rank level and responsibility. Disappointment in command is an important psychological event that ultimately leaves the soldier feeling more vulnerable in a threatening environment. Exploring this in the session can be filled with projections and displacements that need to be worked through to locate the client's distorted ideal. When the therapist finds the distorted ideal, it is important to recognize that this is a fragile component of the client's self-ideal that he or she struggles to identify and does not always recognize as needing to be worked through. It is a challenge to process how the client has shifted the self-ideal due to the way he or she has internalized his or her command. The data also indicate that the importance of disappointment and disruptions in primary spousal and family relationships adds to a deep sense of disorganization and lack of anchoring to a psychological center.

In conclusion, it often takes considerable time in treatment before discrete events are brought into the treatment relationship by the soldier on his or her psychological time frame in order to deepen a sustaining/organizing transference. This indicates that the therapeutic relationship is able to help the soldier manage the effects associated with the impact of the ruptures in relationships with his or her spouse, children, friends, or command. Facing painful and disorganizing affects in treatment may lead to an ability to approach discrete events with a greater sense of confidence that these events may be approached on manifest and latent levels.

Future Research

In looking at future research, it is indicated that the population used for grounded theory does not require a large sample size. The qualitative research method provided rich insight into the deeper emotional experience of the participants. Future research based on the findings of this study should take the current categories of this study and turn them into a survey instrument. Results could be obtained from distribution to a larger population, either in the same Combat Arms or a broader population that would include different branches of the military. In addition, an instrument based on the results of this study could be designed to determine how the population ranks them in importance.

Appendix A
Informed Consent

Appendix A
Informed Consent

Individual Consent for Participation in Research

INSTITUTE FOR CLINICAL SOCIAL WORK

I, _____, acting for myself
(or for my child _____), agree
to take part in the research entitled: "Exploring the meaning of the self
expression of a combat soldier's definition of being "broken"."

This work will be carried out by <u>Bobbie Davis, LCSW</u> (Principal Researcher)
under the supervision of <u>Dennis Shelby, Ph.D., and James Lampe, Ph.D.</u>
(Dissertation Chair and Sponsoring Faculty)

Purpose
The purpose of this study is to explore, by interview, what it means to a
soldier to identify them as broken. This term is created by the soldiers; the
use of the word carries a lot of psychological meaning and other concepts
within, significance and objective.

PROCEDURES USED IN THE STUDY AND THE DURATION

This research is being conducted by face-to-face interview. The interview
should last approximately 45 minutes. Questions in the interview are open
ended allowing the Subject to answer freely. The interview will be recorded
with a digital recorder, later to be transcribed by the researcher for later
data analysis.

Benefits

The benefit is in the outcomes of the research. The analysis of the data has
potential to provide rich understanding and meaning to the experience of

a soldier who identifies themselves as broken. This can aid professions in the mental health field in broadening perspective in providing treatment to a soldier who feels they are broken.

Costs

There are no costs related to this research to either the Subject or for the researcher.

Possible Risks and/or Side Effects

The risk in this research cannot be predicted. If any adverse reaction should occur during the process, the research will assist the Subject in obtaining services through the Emergency Behavioral Health Program, by being assisted in obtaining a therapist who can assist in the reaction the subject experiences.

Privacy and Confidentiality

The identity of the subject will remain confidential. The interview and other material that pertains to the subject will be coded. After the interview is transcribed the digital recording will be deleted. The identifiable materials will be kept in a locked file cabinet until the research is completed. After completion of the research the identifiable material will be shredded and disposed of.

Subject Assurances

By signing this consent form, I agree to take part in this study. I have not given up any of my rights (my child's rights) or released this institution from responsibility for carelessness.

I may cancel my consent and refuse to continue in this study (or take my child out of this study) at any time without penalty or loss of benefits. My relationship with the staff of the ICSW will not be affected in any way, now or in the future, if I (or my child) refuse to take part, or if I begin the study and then withdraw.

If I (or my child) have any questions about the research methods, I can contact <u>Bobbie Davis, LCSW</u> (Principal Researcher) or <u>James Lampe, Ph.D.</u> (Dissertation Chair/Sponsoring Faculty), at this phone number <u>(270)-798-4269</u> (day), <u>(931)-436-3683</u> (evening).

If I have any questions about my rights – or my child's rights – as a research subject, I may contact Daniel Rosenfeld, Chair of Institutional Review Board; ICSW; 401 South State Street Suite 822; Chicago, IL 60605; (312) 935-4232.

Signatures

I have read this consent form and I agree to take part (or, to have my child take part) in this study as it is explained in this consent form.

_____ _____

Signature of Participant   Date

_____ _____

Signature of child (if over 10 years)   Date

I certify that I have explained the research to _____ (Name of subject or child) and believe that they understand and that they have agreed to participate freely. I agree to answer any additional questions when they arise during the research or afterward.

_____ _____

Signature of Researcher   Date

Revised 6 Sep 2006

Appendix B
Interview Questions

Appendix B
Interview Questions

First Interview Questions:

Have you been deployed, and if so where and when did you deploy?

How many times have you deployed?

Have you referred to yourself as being broken?

Appendix C
Demographics Questions

Appendix C
Demographics Questions

The next group of questions deals with some background information about you and your household. This information is needed in order to group your responses with those of persons with a similar background when the results of this study are analyzed.

1. What is your age?

2. _____What is your sex?

Male 1
Female 2

3. Which <u>one</u> of these groups would you say <u>best</u> describes your racial background?

American Indian or Alaska Native 1
Asian...2
Black or African American 3
Native Hawaiian or Other Pacific Islander 4
White 5
Something else *(Please write-in below)* 6

Don't know/Not sure 7
Refuse to answer 8

4. What is your MOS and Rank?

5. What is your present marital status?

Married 1
Living with a partner 2
Separated or divorced 3

Appendix D
Risk Assessment Questionnaire

Appendix D
Risk Assessment Questionnaire

Risk Assessment Questionnaire (Asked at the beginning of the second interview):

Suicidal ideation?
Suicidal plans?
Suicidal intent?

Homicidal ideations?
Homicidal plans?
Homicidal intent?

Dangerousness assessment: Suicide Risk and Protective Factors Review:

Non-Modifiable:
Gender (risk factor if male):
H/O Suicide Attempts: as a teenager:
Organized Plan:
Chronic Psychiatric Disorder:
Recent Psychiatric Hospitalization:
H/O Abuse or Trauma:
Chronic Physical Illness:
Family H/O Suicide/Attempts:
Other Recent Loss:
Chronic Pain:
Age (risk factor if <25 or >60):

Modifiable:
Suicidal ideation/plans/intent:
Access to Lethal Means:
Poor Treatment Compliance:

Hopelessness:
Psychic Pain/Anxiety:
Acute Event:
Insomnia:
Low Self-Worth:
Impulsivity:
Substance Abuse:
Financial Stress:
Legal Stress:

Protective:
Strong Therapeutic Alliance:
Positive Coping Skills:
Responsible to/for Family:
Responsible to/for Pet:
Frustration Tolerance:
Resilience:
Good Reality Testing:
Amenable to Treatment:
Social Support:
Religious Beliefs Contrary to Suicide:

Risk of Harm to Others:

Action Taken Based on Risk Assessment:

[] Released without limitations. Advised of emergency procedures.
[] SM released to Chain of Command with the following limitations:
[] SM sent to ER for evaluation for admission to inpatient psychiatry
[] Other:

Appendix E
Letter of Support

Appendix E
Recruitment Flyer

Appendix F
Recruitment Flyer

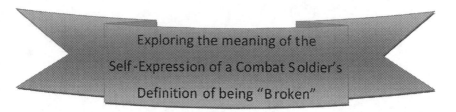

Exploring the meaning of the
Self-Expression of a Combat Soldier's
Definition of being "Broken"

Student researcher at The Institute for Clinical Social Work wants to find the meaning of the self-expression of "Broken". This research study is for Soldiers who have combat experience and defined themselves as "Broken".

Research is always voluntary!

Would the study be a good fit for me?
This study might be a good fit for you if:

- Active Duty or Prior Service with Combat Experience
- Deployment in either Iraq or Afghanistan, with combat experience
- Referred to yourself as being broken

What would happen if I took part in the study?
If you decide to take part in the research study, you would:

- Phone interview with researcher to meet criteria
- Three Face to Face 45 min interviews by Skype or ooVoo ☺ Discuss the Impact of combat experience

What are the benefits if I took part in the study?

The possible benefits if you take part in the study:

- Outcome provides understanding of the combat Soldiers Experience of being broken
- Aid professionals in the mental health field in providing treatment for Soldiers

To take part in research study or for more information, please contact Ms. Bobbie Davis, LCSW at Email: <u>bobbie.davis@me.com</u> or phone: 931-436-3683

THE INSTITUTE FOR
Clinical Social Work

References

American Psychiatric Association. (2000). *Diagnostic and statistical manual of mental disorders* (4th ed., text rev.). Washington, DC: Author.

Boulanger, G. (2007). *Wounded by reality: Understanding and treating adult onset trauma.* New York: Psychology Press.

Corbin, J., & Strauss, A. (2008). *Basics of qualitative research* (3rd ed.). Thousand Oaks, CA: Sage Publications.

Creswell, J. W. (2007). *Qualitative inquiry & research design: Choosing among five approaches* (2nd ed.). Thousand Oaks, CA: Sage Publications.

Davis, B. (2012). *Exploring the psychological meaning of the experience of combat soldiers that have defined themselves as being "broken"* [Unpublished paper]. The Institute for Clinical Social Work, Chicago, Illinois.

Dilthey, W. (1986). The understanding of other persons and their life-expressions. In K. Mueller Vollmer (Ed.), *The hermeneutic reader: Texts of the German tradition from the enlightenment to the present.* London: Basil Blackwell.

Fairbairn, W. D. (1952). *Psychoanalytic studies of the personality.* London: Tavistock Publications Limited.

Freud, S. (1913). *Totem and taboo: Some points of agreement between the mental lives of savages and neurotics.*

Freud, S. (1915). *Thoughts for the times on war and death. The standard edition of the complete psychological works of Sigmund Freud.*

Freud, S. (1917). *Mourning and melancholia. The standard edition of the complete psychological works of Sigmund Freud, Volume XIV (1914-1916).*

Freud, S. (1961). *Beyond the pleasure principle.* In J. Strachey (Ed.), *The standard edition of the complete psychological works of Sigmund Freud, Volume XVIII,* pp. 1-64. London: Hogarth Press.

Freud, S. (1961). New introductory lectures on psycho-analysis. In J. Strachey (Ed.), *The standard edition of the complete psychological works of Sigmund Freud, Volume XV*. London: Hogarth Press.

Glasser, B., & Strauss, A. (1967). *The discovery of grounded theory*. New Brunswick, NJ: Aldine Transaction

Hartmann, H. (1959). Psychoanalysis as a scientific theory. In S. Hook (Ed.), *Psychoanalysis, scientific method and philosophy*. New York: New York University Press.

Kardiner, A. (1941). *The traumatic neuroses of war*. New York: Paul B. Hoeber.

Kime, P. (2012). Army faces highest monthly total suicides. *Army Times*.

Kohut, H. (1971). *The analysis of the self*. New York: International Universities Press.

Kohut, H. (1977). The Oedipus complex and the psychology of the self. In *The restoration of the self*. New York: International Universities Press.

Kohut, H. (1978). Reflections on advances in self psychology. In P. Ornstein (Ed.), *The search for the self* (Vol. 3, pp. 261-357). New York International Universities Press.

Kohut, H. (1982). Introspection, empathy, and the semi-circle of mental health. *International Journal of Psycho-Analysis*.

Kohut, H. (1984). *How does analysis cure?* Chicago: Chicago University of Chicago Press.

Kohut, H., & Wolf, E. S. (1978). The disorders of the self and their treatment: An outline. *International Journal of Psycho-Analysis, 59,* 413-425.

Niederland, W. G. (1968). In H. G. Krystal (Ed.), *Massive psychic trauma*. New York: International Universities Press

Ornstein, A. (1994). Chapter 9: Trauma, memory, and psychic continuity. *Progress in Self Psychology, 10,* 131-146.

Rasmussen, B. (2013). The effects of trauma treatment on the therapist. In S. Ringell & J. Brandell (Eds.), *Trauma: Contemporary directions in theory, practice and research* (pp. 223-246). Thousand Oaks, CA: Sage Publications.

Remarque, E. (1928). *All quiet on the western front*. New York: Fawcett.

Shelby, R. D. (1990). *If a partner has AIDS*. Binghampton, NY: The Haworth Press.

Shelby, R. D. (2000). Use of the mentoring relationship to facilitate rigor in qualitative research. *Smith College Studies in Social Work, 7*(2).

Shelby, R. D., & Roldan, I. (2004). Mentoring. In D. Padgett (Ed.), *The qualitative research experience.* Florence, KY: Wadsworth Thompson

Siegel, A. (1996). *Heinz Kohut and the psychology of the self.* New York.

Stolorow, R. D. (2007). Chapter 3: The phenomenology of trauma and the absolutisms of everyday life in trauma and human existence: Autobiographical, psychoanalytic, and philosophical reflections. *Psychoanalytic Inquiry Book Series, 23.*

Stolorow, R. D., Atwood, G. E., & Orange, D. M. (2002). *Chapter 7: Worlds of trauma in worlds of experience: Interweaving philosophical and clinical dimensions in psychoanalysis.* New York: Basic Books.

Strauss, A., & Corbin, J. (2008). *Basics of qualitative research: Techniques and procedures for developing grounded theory* (2nd ed.). Thousand Oaks, CA: Sage Publications.

Thompson, M., & Gibbs, N. (2012). *Time Magazine.*

Tolpin, M. (2002). Doing psychoanalysis of normal development: Forward edge transferences. *Progress in Self Psychology, 18,* 167-190.

Ulman, R. B., & Brothers, D. (1987). A self-psychological reevaluation of Posttraumatic Stress Disorder (PTSD) and its treatment. *Journal of the American Academy of Psychoanalysis, 15,* 175-203.

U. S. Department of Defense. Army release august suicide data. Retrieved August, 2012 from http://www.defense.gov/Releases/Release. aspx?ReleaseID=15588

Williamson, V., & Mulhall, E. (2009, January). Invisible wounds: Psychological and neurological injuries confront a new generation of veterans. *Issue Report.* Iraq and Afghanistan Veterans of America.

Wolf, E. S. (1995). Psychic trauma: A view from self psychology. *Canadian Journal of Psychoanalysis, 3,* 203-222.

Printed in the United States
By Bookmasters